Marty -

Norm is a good friend of mine.
He was in country at the same
Time I was. He received the
Navy Cross for his actions after
he team was ambushed.

Semper Fi

Rod

SWIFT

SILENT

DEADLY

Norman VanCor

ISBN 978-1-62806-298-4 (print | hardback)

Library of Congress Control Number 2020919789

Published by Salt Water Media
29 Broad Street, Suite 104
Berlin, MD 21811
www.saltwatermedia.com

Interior images provided by the author

Neither the United States Marine Corps nor any other component of the Department of Defense has approved, endorsed, or authorized this book.

February 18, 1968

"The duty of peace is burdensome. It is a duty many generations of Americans have chosen as their own. It is a duty many other young men have borne as you bear it now. In the discharge of that duty, none have honored themselves – none have honored their nation – so nobly, or so bravely, as the United States Marines."

President Lyndon B. Johnson
To Marines leaving for Viet Nam

I dedicate this book, with the unfolding of my Marine Corps life, as testimony to and an accounting of my experience as a young man at war in Viet Nam, to my two wonderful daughters whom I love and adore.

Christine Marie
Kimberly Grace

And to honor the memory of *First Lieutenant John M. Shinault* (left) and *Corporal Daniel Tirado* (right).

Memorial Service for First Lieutenant John Shinault and Corporal Danny Tirado

Viet Nam Memorial

The black marble slabs look sterile and pure,
Like asking forgiveness or seeking a cure.
The tiny names inscribed by the score,
Lined up neatly in rows forever more.

The ominous black marble is impressive to see,
It brings back memories and emotions, hoping to go free.
Trapped in a monument for the nation to ponder,
A legacy of death, lost souls that wander.

The helicopters roar, the tracers fly, and the grenades explode,
Sounds of death so distant, where the red blood flowed.
People leave things at The Wall, and cry and stare,
Like at a grave, they lay their feelings bare.

Back out of the jungle they came, zipped up neatly in a bag,
Sent home to their loved ones, kept track of by a tag.
Fighting a war for they knew not why,
Knowing full well, they'd probably die.

All have their reason to visit The Wall,
Most are personal, others a curiosity call.
No matter who visits that National site,
They can't help but leave, feeling somewhat contrite.

Norman W. VanCor
July 19, 1992

CONTENTS

PREFACE

When I was in my sixties, I developed a keen interest in reading the history of the Viet Nam war. Everyone seemed more interested in it and its veterans, maybe because there was the vantage point of two generations of guilt over it. Or maybe, it was a morbid fascination with the whole thing that transcends the ugly protests and disdain for those of us once considered murderers, rapists and baby killers. These days, folks want to shake my hand and say "thank you for your service." They are mostly the sons and daughters of my comrades or others who just want to make amends for the injustice and anger that was so freely dispensed and heaped upon us as soldiers and returning veterans.

I wanted to read and research the truth, the real history of the politics of the time and the true events and decision-making that took place in Washington during the war years.

So far, it is sad commentary; history reveals so much correlation between what we began to realize so long ago while sitting on sandbags in Quang Tri with what was actually happening here at home. It is frightening to imagine what we had to do to satisfy the ambitions of incompetent generals and presidents. It is sinful, and, in rare moments, reading that stuff has made me weep.

All of the good intentions to prevent the spread of communism across Southeast Asia and beyond, all of the "truth, honor and the American way" slogans that we warriors fought and died for, and the pride of being a Marine Recon warrior, was all for naught. No one really cared except for the families. And then there were the other families that gathered for another funeral. Who cared about them? Was it LBJ? General Westmoreland? Robert McNamara? No, none of them cared. My first sergeant cared and so did we of 3-C-2.

We were pretty much alone, sent to the Pointless Forest in a game of death and body count math.

I'm not so much bitter as I am dismayed and let down by the people I looked up to the most. They were our leaders, the admired wise men that we could depend on to guide us to victory. On Memorial Day, I could proudly march down Main Street, Ashfield, Massachusetts, with the elders from the Greatest Generation to the cemetery to pay homage to our fallen brethren. My dad would be proud. Mr. Whitney would invite me to carry the flag.

Nah, never happened.

Why would they let a baby killer carry the flag? Most of the Viet Nam vets threw out their uniforms or hid them in a closet.

But it's changed now. In a world of better understanding, we have been forgiven for being a Marine at war, sent by the same Uncle Sam that called to duty millions of Americans since our Colonial days. I don't want anyone to change history, only to accurately describe it.

I don't pretend that this book is anywhere near a history of the war in Viet Nam, just the story of one who fought in it. There are thousands of stories like my own. But it helps me, and maybe you, better understand what went on during that time and in that place.

INTRODUCTION

Friends, acquaintances, and even a member of the Third Recon Battalion Association, have encouraged me to write a book about my time in Viet Nam. My response has always been the same, "The world doesn't need another war story."

There have been many things on my mind these last few months that prompted me to change my thinking about a book. Maybe it was the realization of age. Turning 70 years old can have a sobering influence on prioritizing those things that you choose to do or put off. My health is all right, but one look at the obituary page and one wonders where I might fit into the grand scheme of God's plan for me.

And then, there is the number of years since I was in Viet Nam. The year 2018 was the 50-year anniversary since I first set foot on the tarmac of Da Nang City on that dark, rainy night in 1968. Good Lord Almighty, where, oh where, has the time gone! There's also the argument that my story is more than the blood and guts war story. I've tried to emphasize the human thinking and personal feelings into the terror of jungle warfare.

I provided a partial exploration of combat, living conditions and food, at the Recon Base Camp in Quang Tri in a taped interview I did for the "Library of Congress Veterans' Living History Project." It was conducted some years ago at Central Connecticut State University for the documentation and preservation of first-hand stories of veterans of all wars. Particular emphasis was placed on World War II, Korea and Viet Nam. It is important to document actual accounts of the wars while veterans are still alive and able to tell our stories.

After I returned home from Viet Nam and until my father's death in 2002, my dad and I never really talked much about war. In those 33 years, we never once asked each other direct questions about the blood and guts aspect of war. We chewed around the edges a little by talking about the countryside, living on C-rations and sleeping on the ground. But we never compared notes on what nightmares are made of.

My two wonderful children, Christine and Kimberly, know very little about that part of my life. Their children, my grandkids, Giana, Sophie and Gavin will someday want to know, I'm sure.

People everywhere should listen to the veterans and read first-hand accounts of those of us who experienced war and the destructive and senseless impact war has on a society.

I must stress that the accounts in this book are as accurate and true as my memory allows. There are certain profound events in everyone's lives that remain clear, if not vivid. I believe I have conveyed an accurate description of the facts of my experience in Viet Nam. I have relied on my memory. I have not researched history chronicles or asked other vets for their thoughts. I make no attempt to chronicle every event or firefight with the enemy. Many missions were mundane and repetitive. Those missions were no less scary, just routine. We walked point for the grunts and sometimes we made mistakes, not adhering to trained discipline. Sometimes Lady Luck steers fate. This book is my own. It is not a Recon story or a Marine Corps war story. This book is my story.

There is some dialogue in this book in quotes, but, of course, in most cases, I cannot possibly remember exactly what was said. Rather, I have tried to convey the personality and character of the individuals. There are no apologies for some of the salty language. That, too, must be accepted as the way it was. I made several references to my team (3-C-2) as being good - damned good, tight, and other such terms to denote some sort of superiority. I did not intend a braggart tone, but rather to illustrate our mental need to convince ourselves that we could get through the next mission. Without confidence and even a little swagger, we would have been demoralized. Mission after endless mission took a mental toll and we had to maintain confidence and some sort of competitive edge within our company to avoid low morale and a defeatist attitude. I hope that makes some sense to the reader.

My wife, Elaine, supported the idea of a book and encouraged me to keep going. She, more than anyone, gave me the ardency to continue and complete my legacy to family and beyond. Without her tremendous assistance in transcribing, and her suggestions, large and small, I would have been lost. And, I must also give warm thanks to my friend, author and editor, John McGauley. His advice and thought-provoking questions and comments have been an immeasurable help to me.

It is done. I have made a sincere and honest attempt to capture the experiences, both physically and mentally, of one Recon Marine sent to the land of Viet Nam to be thrust into the hostile, hot, steamy jungles; to be hunted by enemy forces, animals, insects and the natural elements. Exposed nerves, fear, clear thinking, all played a vital role in everything we did. The overpowering desire to stay alive, to kill or be killed dominated my mind. Helicopter extractions from a hot LZ, ear-blowing grenade explosions and the terror of AK-47's and M-16's on full automatic in a firefight with NVA was real. It was up close and personal. It had all the ingredients for a lifetime of haunting nightmares. Welcome to war in Viet Nam – hell begins here.

CHAPTER 1

Cruising along at 400 mph and 30,000 feet above the ground, I somehow felt safe. There was no flak, no tail-gunner, no bombs to unload. It was just a quiet trip from a California airbase to Da Nang, South Vietnam. It was just us, 80 guys. The one thing we had in common was that we were all Marine Corps trained killing machines on our way to kick ass until all the gook asses had been kicked. Then we'd go home.

That's what I thought with my head laid back against a soft pillow. Dim lights on a dark night somewhere over the Pacific Ocean was the setting. I suddenly realized it was quiet, very quiet for a plane full of Marines. The overhead reading lights were on here and there but no one had a book. I observed no one was asleep although some pretended to be or wanted to be. Some guys were staring into nothing, some guys fidgeted and no one said a word. We all knew we were being hurled at 400 mph to a destiny somewhere in a faraway land called Nam.

I couldn't help but think back on the day I visited First Sergeant Clem Record right near the Greenfield Community College campus. Record was the local USMC recruiter. He lived just up the street from us in Ashfield, Massachuetts. I even kissed his daughter once but I hope he didn't know.

He was happy to see me and even jovial when I expressed my desire to join his beloved Corps. He downright loved the idea and the paperwork was begun. I could go to Parris Island soon and become a

United States Marine. Hoo-rah!

Our descent into Da Nang was uneventful. Still no flak. We bounced around some and could hear the pounding rain beating at us like a threat. Stairs were rolled over and a first lieutenant in a slicker barked at us to do this and that and go to the Headquarters tent. I stood up straight and stretched while adjusting my nicely starched utility trousers. I adjusted my starched cover and started for the door.

By God, we're here, let's get it on, I recall thinking.

All our seabags were removed from cargo. We were told to just grab one and go. Holy shit, was it raining. I was soaked to the skin before I hit the second step and could hardly make it out to the tarmac. I had never been in rain that hard. The white starch rolled down my skin and I was left with limp and wet trousers, shirt and cover. It was miserable.

The big tent reminded me of a circus big top. It was huge and chaotic with the ringmaster barking at full strength. Bring your orders here, go there after, no grabass, you'll be here till daybreak, grab a bunk. Bunk? What bunk? There were several rows of sagging springs hanging from iron posts. I guess that's them. Someone remarked on the thunder. The ringmaster blared out, "That's not thunder, shit-for-brains, that's incoming mortar. Christ, where do they get these idiots!"

So, soaked to the bones and now cold, I wasn't about to flop on bare sagging springs, so I just stood there. After some time, I began to dry and the starch had glued my clothes to my skin. If I wasn't so scared, I might have laughed. I was starting to realize just where I was and why. The sound of the mortar rounds didn't help. It was November 10, 1968, the Marine Corps birthday.

I had no way of knowing at the time, but that night, my first night in the big top, would be the safest I would be for the next thirteen months. I was very quickly going to be in harm's way.

CHAPTER 2

Finally, it was dawn. Well, it was sort of dawn. There was a little light, but the torrents of rain were relentless. There were a few cases of C-rations in the corner where we were instructed to get at it if we wanted chow. Someone gave me a P-38 to open my can of fruit cocktail. A P-38 is a clever little tool about an inch long that has a flip-out point. Once you get the hang of it, you can zip open a can in a jiff. Some of the hot shots tried to show off just how fast they could open a can. And some slopped the contents on the wet tarmac floor. Of course, the ringmaster barked at them for that.

"OK, listen up," barked the ringmaster. "I'm going to call your name once. When I do, get your scrawny ass up here and get your orders. I will tell you once which 6-by to get in. The first group will get in that truck right out there. You're going to 1-9, you poor bastards. Lucas...Schultz...Rooney... and on he went, about ten in all.

Then he went to the next group and the next. As trucks left and others pulled up, I got more concerned. I knew I was going to Third Recon. During combat infantry training at Camp Pendleton, I was reassigned to a group training separately. It was more intense and definitely more advanced. I trained as a radio operator in San Diego and was top in my class. Big deal. It wasn't that hard. But I didn't see any of the other guys here that I trained with.

"OK, listen up," he shouted again, "all you other gook bait are going to headquarters from here to Con Tien" and he rattled off the names.

I was the last name he called, the very last!

"Okay, VanCor, where are you?"

"Here," I shouted back.

"Okay, your sorry ass is going to Quang Tri to Recon. You poor bastard. Get in that truck with those guys."

I didn't even know what "Recon" meant until boot camp. It is the special forces of the Marine Corps...the toughest of the tough... the Navy Seal program was modeled after Recon. But the thought lingered with me that if Recon Marines were that bad-ass, why did they pick me? Every unit gets a token mulligan, I figured.

So, I went, seabag over my shoulder, up and over the big-ass tailgate on the truck. Once again, I was soaked and cold to the bone. I found a spot and slipped down to the hard truck bed and we began our 90-mile journey, slogging and slopping our way up the road. The rain was deafening. It hit me so hard it hurt. I just sat and stared ahead, no rifle, no food, nothing but my thoughts of home and what I might be doing if I were there. Oh, if only I were there. Hell, I didn't even know what day it was or what time it was at home.

I would soon find out, up close and personal, that rain, cold, mud and no food weren't my enemy; I would forget about those things; I would deal with it. I'd learn to adapt, improvise and overcome. I'd learn how to become a Recon Marine. I just didn't know it yet.

Hour by hour we went ahead but nothing changed. There were countless rice fields with water buffalo standing in them. They were the farmers' friends and livelihood, and months later when I would see guys shoot water buffalo for sport and then laugh, I'd get sick and wish I wasn't with them. They were grunts (infantry) we were with, not Recon. No wonder the farmers and villagers learned to hate Americans.

Finally, I was the last guy on the truck; the last guy before me had jumped off and yelled, "She's all yours now, Recon," and as he swaggered away with his seabag, he slipped and fell sideways in the mud. It was then that I laughed. The "she" that my muddy friend referred to was a 60-caliber machine gun mounted on the roof with a band of ammo leading down to a wooden case of 500 rounds. It was time to stand up anyway. I stood spread eagled to steady myself and looked ahead at the treeline.

What desolate wasteland, I thought. Haphazard mounds and a small raised vault with a cross atop gave evidence of a Christian cemetery. Huge flooded fields with straight water-filled canals supported little sprouts of newly planted rice was my guess. More barren land tangled up in brush gave way to woodland but there were no good trees in there, just a jumble of brush, vines and tall twisted dead trunks. It looked ominous.

A long fenceline lay ahead with coil upon coil of concertina wire and beyond that were jeeps and trucks and rows of tents, then there was a bunch of plywood pieces pretending to be a building with a large American flag hanging limply, dripping with water. Finally, through the gate we went and we came to a stop, the truck wheels settling in the mud.

The company clerk looked very busy but was expecting me. He yelled out to the first sergeant that "the replacement is here."

Holy shit! The first sergeant was a giant of a man full of muscle and grit and he looked down on me as you would view a dead rat.

"So," he says, "Where the fuck have you been?"

"I've been on that truck and ..."

"Why didn't you get a chopper? Christ, boy...oh never mind... you're here now," he spat out. I could see that he didn't like me at all but weeks later I would learn that he was a gentle giant who loved us all. He would die with us or for us. He would commandeer supplies for us and resort to thievery if it would help us. He was "The Man."

Leaving the supply shack with a poncho over me, an armload of dry fatigues underneath, a seabag over my shoulder and a metal tray, cup and utensils banging and clanging, I splashed my way down the mud path to a large tent with a little painted 3C2 (Third Platoon, Charlie Company, Team 2). Here I am. Quang Tri Base Camp. It's a spitting distance to the DMZ with a Battalion of Recon Marines in old canvas tents, although there were several plywood "hooches" with metal roofs.

My eyes adjusted to the dark interior of the tent. Two hanging flashlights illuminated four guys sitting around a foot locker playing cards. With barely a glance, one guy asked, "Do you know how to play poker?"

"No," I replied, "Never learned."

"Hope the fuck he knows how to use a Prick-25," another guy half asked, half chuckled, The PRC-25 is a multi-frequency radio carried in a backpack with an 18" flexible antenna and a transmitting range of 25 miles. He was using the slang term for the only communications device we would have on missions.

Screw them, I thought. I dumped my gear down by the one empty cot. It was the old scissor type canvas cot similar to what was used in the officers' tents during the Civil War. Left over, no doubt.

I peeled off my wet clothes into a pile and put on dry ones. There was a poncho liner which was used as a blanket during the rainy season. No pillow, of course. So I bunched up a pair of trousers and stretched out. I'll go right to sleep.

In the background, I could hear the same repetitive boom-boom-boom that I later learned was our artillery sending out 155 howitzer love notes to the North Vietnamese Army.

Man, what a day. It sucked, not what I expected at all. I hadn't eaten all day.

There would be many more of those days in the months ahead. And, there would be those guys. Very soon I would love them and them me. We would trust each other with our lives. We would be alone, just us five, in a hostile jungle engaged in a firefight. Every minor move we made would have life or death consequences. Tonight, they knew that but I didn't. I slept a deep sleep uninterrupted by nightmares of automatic AK-47 gunfire and NVA voices in the jungle nights that terrified the soul. The 20-year-old lad from Massachusetts, the naïve Recon Marine, slept.

 CHAPTER 3

I awoke with a start. Oh yeah, I was in a musty-smelling, rotten tent, on a Civil War cot. I sat upright.

"Well, good morning, boot camp, decide to wake up? Ready for your breakfast in bed?" Mex said.

"Fuck you, asshole," I replied. They all laughed.

"Welcome to Viet Nam, bro," Mex said.

The team leader, John, threw a flimsy empty pack in my direction and told me we were going for a little stroll.

Outside, I had to squint, the rising sun was already hot and the air was steamy. The mud from all the rain was starting to bake dry.

Big Bart hoisted a full sand bag into my pack and away we went, each taking a bag of sand for a jog.

The sand bag didn't take long to get a little heavy, but there were no complaints from me. "What's the deal with the piles of sand?" I asked. There wasn't much to do in base camp in between missions. One occupation of time was to fill sand bags and place around the tents. There was occasional mortar incoming and the sand bags helped. There was a big hopper to catch a shovel full of sand with a funnel arrangement at the bottom. One guy shoveled sand, one guy held an empty bag under the funnel, another guy got the bag when full and tied a good knot at the top and the other two guys stacked the bags. The first sergeant kept a whole team busy for hours playing in the sand.

Our run went on for miles. Someone said three but it seemed like ten. Back at our comfy little tent, we grabbed our metal tray with a wire through the corner, which also went through the fork, spoon and tin cup, clanging up the dried-mud street past all the other tents and hooches in Charlie Company towards the mess hall. Standing in line, I was told not to bitch about the food.

The food was hot, the coffee was weak and the bread had been fresh at some point but not that day or even that week. Everything was powdered and reconstituted with iodine laced water. But at least it wasn't cold C-rations. I learned why the wire was on the tray. Two 50-gallon metal drums were outside. One had hot soapy water and the other had less soapy hot water. Holding the wire, we simply dipped our trays and utensils in the first barrel a few times. The second barrel, the rinse barrel, took off some of the soap. We walked away with the whole rig to drip dry as we clanged our way back to our tent.

The next few days were spent listening, bonding and asking questions.

I needed to practice with my new M-16 rifle since I had never fired one before. In boot camp, we qualified on the range with the older M-14 rifle. The newer M-16 rifle was experimental and first used in Viet Nam. I field-stripped the new rifle several times, and learned to put only 18 rounds in the magazine, not 20, to avoid jamming. I learned to keep the springs clean in the magazine and to always tape the end of the barrel to keep out mud and water. I learned never ever do this, don't forget to do that and, above all, remember this or that. John, as team leader, really took me under his wing the most, and spent quite a bit of time teaching me how to construct my harness to my new backpack. Like suspenders, the harness was constructed using used pieces of webbing and straps from the supply hut. Everything had a place to belong. We each carried two grenades and one smoke cannister, which hung on the harness. Attached on the web belt was 25 magazines of ammo taped end to end for quick exchange and five canteens of water (one for each day).

It's a good thing we had many deep pockets on our camouflage trousers; they were filled with goodies such as battle dressings, body paint from a lipstick-like container in a dark greenish-black color. The idea was to blend into the jungle.

We also carried many salt tablets. We needed them with the temperatures climbing to over 100° and 90% humidity. With a limit of five canteens of water, personal restraint was a must. We each carried iodine tabs in case we got stuck out there and had to drink swamp water.

We all carried a razor-sharp K-bar (a large U.S.-issued hunting knife and sheath). Some guys had their own handguns because government-issued 45 caliber pistols were hard to come by; the Army guys got those. The only new gear I got was boots, two sets of utilities (civilians call them pants and shirts) and socks. I scrounged the rest. My rifle was newer but not new.

Recon Marines didn't wear helmets and flak jackets. We acquired soft, brimless covers (which civilians call hats).

Packing one's pack – that was another thing to learn and that was very serious business. With five Recon Marines out in the jungle on a mission, noise is a life-and-death deal. Before going out, we went to the ammo dump and got fresh bandoliers of ammo to load up and a case of C-rats (rations). Most of the case was wasted and given to the garbage dump which the villagers from Con Tien, a couple of miles away, would scavage. The only food we took was the pound cake and fruit cocktail, peaches or pear tins. There was no cooking, of course, and the reason we left the other stuff at the dump was because it had lard and gristle and was disgusting to eat, hot or cold. It was crucial to tape the cans together to avoid having them rattle around. Silence and stealth were uppermost in our minds, constantly.

Missions were typically five days and we ate a little twice per day. Our minds were occupied by matters more important than food. Cigarettes and gum were prohibited, along with anything that smelled, made noise or wasn't absolutely necessary. Even a small roll of white toilet paper was forbidden.

Our packs were light and versatile. We carried no extra clothes or a poncho. Rain hitting plastic ponchos made too much noise. Besides, we were never dry anyway.

Ah, and then there was my radio. At the Comm shack, I learned stuff about the PR-25 that I sure wasn't taught in school. There was a small handset attached to a rubber cord and a knob for frequency settings and squelch control that always acted finicky. Inside was a battery about the size of two bricks and about as heavy and I also carried a spare battery sealed in a thick plastic bag. In the jungle, all empty cans, used batteries and any trash was covered with ground litter because we carried no entrenchment tool.

And then there were the I-A drills which stood for "immediate action drills." We practiced every day. There was always a specific order of movement. Bart, our point man, was first and he used a green twine to tie to the end of the rifle barrel and sling over his shoulder so his rifle was always up and at the ready.

Bart had no fear and, I swear, if he would have been shot, ice water would have oozed out. I never did know his last name but I heard his first name was Bartholomew and I knew I would never utter his full name. He was one tough hombre and commanded respect and admiration from all of us for his keen senses and steady hands. We moved at his pace.

Next, and about five to six feet behind Bart, was our team leader, John Simineau. He was a corporal on his second tour. He was a little squirrelly but the best man you'd ever want on your side of a fight.

I was next. I was the radio man. I was untested, the new guy, the one that no one in his right mind would want to be near in the first firefight.

Behind me was Nick. I think he could have been a Puerto Rican street fighter. He had a rifle and wanted a live target to eliminate. Nick Diaz would never let you down. He would stand his ground. He was a rifleman.

And last came Juan Gaucin, who was the rear security man. This little Mexican was tough as a keg of nails and he carried the M-79, a short-barreled, large-bored weapon that fires a cannister-type round of high explosive. It's like a handheld artillery and quite effective, but obviously not for close-contact firefights. Juan was really good. He could shoot a tennis ball off a flagpole at a hundred yards. He tended to hang back a little to detect if we were being followed.

These I-A drills were intended to practice different movements if we came upon the NVA face-to-face. They consisted of practice using different hand signals, how to disperse, what to do in finding high ground when someone was wounded, all the stuff you needed to know to stay alive.

"Norm, do as I say and exactly as I say and you might live through a firefight. Better yet, you may help me live through it, too," I recall John saying to me several times.

In his second tour, John was hard to figure. He was focused, maybe even a little obsessed with perfection. He wasn't unfriendly but he didn't laugh much or have much fun. He was all business. He acted like the whole war would be won or lost depending on his decisions. One tour of duty, as they called it, would have been enough for that dude.

Early morning on about my fourth day at tent city, the little beady-eyed company clerk stopped by to tell us we're being fragged. That's a term usually referring to the explosion of a hand grenade, but some twisted mind used the term to mean we were being assigned a mission. Some guys called it a patrol but in the official records it's called a mission. No more practice and class. The drills were over for me. It's time to see what I've learned. John and Bart went to the G-2 hut. Those G-2 smart guys were told of a big grunt (infantry) operation maybe or aerial photography caught what looked like a bunker complex or some damned thing that they wanted to send Recon to check out. I went to the Comm shack and checked out a PRC-25 and extra battery. We tested it out and away I went to get a case of C-rats and ammo.

We wouldn't get the smoke cannisters, M-79 rounds and that stuff until we went out the next morning. The ammo dump was near the chopper pad which was over an acre of steel mats linked together by sections to make a strong, flat surface for the helicopters.

The guys were back from G-2. My first mission would be easy, they said, so that was good. "Here's the deal, listen up," John said. "We're taking a 6-by (big ass truck I bounced around on from Da Nang) to Gio

Lin. They're taking incoming every night. We'll be walking in from there to find the little bastards and make them disappear." Easy? Yeah, right, easy.

John gave me a map. We got two, one for me and one for the team leader. It had an oilcloth-type finish and was neatly folded into a small square. It wasn't cut because if we were way out somewhere and got into some shit and had to walk out, we'd have the whole map to find our way out. Or not.

On both maps our area of coverage was framed out in ink. There was an "x" with the word "nuts" written beside it. Whenever I gave our location to the relay station, I referred to "nuts" and right, left, up or down. From "nuts," right 2½, down 1. That placed us in a grid location that was used to keep track of where we were. About twice each day I communicated in a whisper where we were. Our team call sign was "Ringlet." Who knows who dreamed that up. Maybe some guy who is dead now or gone home had a little girl with curly hair. I was given three frequencies: one for the relay station, one for the chopper pilots, and one for fixed wing pilots. After a time, I could reach up behind me and switch frequencies just by feel and not have someone do it for me.

The relay stations were interesting places. Because of the mountainous terrain and jungle canopy, the range of the radio was reduced. Certain mountaintops were strategically chosen to put a relay station with a large antenna and radio to be the go-between for our Comm center and the teams out on missions.

Each relay station was named according to the international phoenetic alphabet. Relay Sierra was ours for this little soiree. If we were walking in or out, an LZ (chopper landing zone) was marked on the map just in case. One of our jobs was to always verify the mapping and the useable LZ's.

The guys always had their own little ritual the night before going out. First, write a letter home. Second, go outside and stare at the moon and stars in silence and think about home. Third, hit the rack (musty, smelly, rotten canvas cot) and think about home.

CHAPTER 4

We hit the chow line early, geared up, including full body camo paint. At 0800, we met our ride to Gio Lin. The air felt good and I was nervous. We all were, but this was all new to me.

When we got to the compound just outside of the village, we looked up the captain in charge. Where did incoming come from, what times, why didn't you call in arty (artillery)? Artillery was our 105 howitzers that were pretty nasty, as I would find out.

I admit, the five of us looked like a pretty tough bunch all loaded and painted up.

I made a radio check and told Sierra that Ringlet was leaving Gio Lin in a northwest direction at 0950, will provide sit rep (situation report) at 1400.

In fifteen minutes, our world changed, the jungle swallowed us and the silence was amazing. I wasn't nervous any more, I was a touch beyond that. I kept telling myself to settle down, relax, get in a rhythm, pay attention. And we did fall into a rhythm. It was incredible how one's body could change so much and so fast. I was on full alert. I chose my steps. My ears and eyes heard and saw everything. I was doing my job. I was finally there and it was happening. I wasn't cooking at Howard Johnson's that day. I wouldn't be going on a date. I wasn't at the table for Mom's dinner or asleep in my clean bed. I was a fuckin' United States Marine - a Recon Marine in a jungle in Viet Nam. There were gooks (NVA Army) out there who would love to kill me and they just could get a chance to do that any minute or maybe the next day. Maybe I'd get a chance to kill them. Yeah, that's a better thought.

The hours dragged by. About every half hour, we would pause and John would point to a spot on his map with his pencil and I would nod. I had us at the same spot. That's good. About 1400 hours John and Bart conferred in a very gentle whisper. We moved on just a little further to a growth of vines with huge leaves.

We sat in a circle as I was taught and leaned against each other to relieve the pressure of our packs. We all sat very still for a while and listened. I then squeezed the handset and whispered, "Sierra, Sierra, this is Ringlet, over."

"Ringlet, this is Sierra, over."

"Location of Ringlet is from nuts, right 7, down 2, all secure, over."

"Roger, copy Ringlet. Time on deck is 1410. Sierra, out."

That was my first report to a relay station. John looked at me and nodded. I felt good. So on it went the rest of the day - walk, pause, sip of water, report, check maps and stay alert. Just before dark we found a good spot to sit and we took turns eating. I muffled the sound of my P-38 tiny can opener as it cut into the metal can. I didn't realize it made so much noise. Putting the can up to my lips to drink the syrup and little pieces of fruit seemed primitive but that's how it was done.

I dug my heel into the soft jungle floor and put the empty can in the hole and covered it over.

Barely before dark, John got us in a kneeling position, nodded his head and looked at a small rise on the ground about 50 yards away.

"Study the route, that's where we're going," he whispered.

An hour after dark, we moved to that small rise without making a noise. We slowly eased into a circle. With rifles on our laps, we settled in for the night. If we heard mortar fire, the hunt would be on and men would die.

Moving after dark to another location was standard Recon practice just in case the enemy had seen where we'd stopped at dusk. I would learn at another time why that was such prudent action. That night, Juan and I had the first watch. Back-to-back, we listened and sat in silence. With the headset near my ear, I faintly heard the voice say, "Ringlet, Ringlet, this is Sierra. Sit-rep."

Silently, I keyed the handset twice. At Sierra relay it would sound like two short squelch noises - chttt, chttt.

"Roger, Ringlet. Time on deck is 2100 hours. Sierra, out."

There would be no talking at night. Juan and I each gave a gentle prod to the man on our left and I passed the handset to him and slumped my head down to doze.

That was a typical day in the land of Nam. We would live another day.

We had a harrowing experience the second night and not from the enemy but our own forces; we took friendly fire dangerously close.

The 105 howitzers were conducting what's called H&I fire, meaning harassment and intradiction. They would fire at coordinates calculated from the previous night where they believed the enemy had fired mortars. We must have been about where the gooks had been the night before.

I more than whispered when I said, "Check fire, check fire! Sierra, this is Ringlet. Tell those assholes to check fire!"

Two more whistles of incoming artillery were above us and then fierce explosions. We were all flat, face down on the jungle floor. Holy shit! We were covered with dirt and debris but no wounds.

And then, it was silent once more. "Sierra, this is Ringlet," I whispered, "All secure."

"Roger, Ringlet. Sorry about that." Somehow they hadn't gotten word we were out there.

The next afternoon we walked out of the jungle on the opposite side of the compound from where we left. Our map and compass did not fail us. The 6-by was waiting and at the ammo dump we offloaded our explosives except for rifle ammo, and five tired guys sloughed off their packs.

It was my first mission. The anticipation was over and I had my first taste of the jungle. It was a world so new to me and frightening. It seemed so hostile and ominous. It was like being swallowed up in another world. There could be no training for that. Knowing where we were, I could see, was going to be a serious task. There were no landmarks, just jungle with places to hide and watch.

CHAPTER 5

The next day would be rifle cleaning, unloading rifle magazines to clean springs and reload. And there were always more sandbags to fill. John and Bart finished debriefing at G-2 so we headed for the showers. With just Marine Corps green skivvies, rubber flip flops made from strips of truck tires and inner tubes, towel and soap, we walked to the central shower. The semi-enclosure consisted of four 50-gallon drums on a platform overhead with plastic refill pipes running to the top. The drums had some nifty device attached to a pull string for the guy standing underneath. The water was non-potable and drawn from the Quang Tri River. The idea was to get wet and use lots of soap and then rinse off. It wasn't very fancy but it worked and felt good. Lingering under the drum was seriously frowned upon.

The heat seemed almost unbearable. It just didn't let up. Every day was 100 degrees or higher and the humidity was so high, it felt like rain. I was dripping wet all the time.

My first guard duty was uneventful. There was no marching back and forth like in the movies. I was assigned to the motor pool from 2400 hours to 0400 hours. I picked a good spot in the cab of some vehicle where I could see the wire in my whole sector. I couldn't be seen in the cab because of the moon reflections on the window.

The worst part of guard duty at night wasn't the staying awake, it was thinking too much.

I still hadn't figured out if it was yesterday or tomorrow at home. Whatever the time, I wanted to be there. All the things I took for granted made me realize how selfish I had become. How my expectations were for everything to go my way, for a nice dinner to magically appear on the table every day at 5 pm.

I started thinking about the team in Delta Company that was attacked at night by a tiger. One guy was dragged off. The tiger was killed and a night extraction was pulled off. The poor guy never had a chance, the tiger had dragged him away by the neck and he was done for.

They'd shot the tiger and brought it back, and its hide was stretched out on a frame for all to see. What does one say to the family of a guy killed in Viet Nam by a tiger? I can't imagine.

I wondered if a military car would pull up in front of my parents' house and an officer and a chaplain would get out and somberly walk to the door. I played out the whole scenario. Too much thinking.

I got my very first helicopter ride two days later. All loaded up for war, Ringlet was out on the chopper pad early.

First, you heard the sound and then you saw it coming down at you. I squeezed the handset and talked with the pilot.

"Huey, this is Ringlet, over."

"Ringlet, this is your ride to Disney, over."

Disney, my ass! A Huey helicopter held a pilot, co-pilot, two gunners with 50-caliber machine guns and a small open cargo deck. As rehearsed, we all ran at once when the helicopter landed, two guys under the props to one side and the other three to the opposite side. The team all crouched and John showed the pilot his map and pointed at the LZ. The pilot confirmed that he had the same coordinates. It was always good to know they didn't pick up the wrong team or take them to the wrong place.

We sat with our legs dangling over the side and away we went. Banking right or left was always a little scary. The deck of the chopper was a smooth, shiny steel and the guy in the middle really needed a hand grip.

I was mesmerized by the jungle canopy below. It looked so smooth in pretty green colors, with valleys rising to steep hills, lots of hills. From so high a vantage point, it was hard to imagine the contrast between the scene from above with a cool breeze on your face and the harsh reality of the scene from the ground, looking up. The cool breeze turned to stifling heat. The valleys were not a pretty green but slime-covered rocks and twisted vines creeping over a tangled rubble of slag and standing putrid water. The helicopter at 1000 feet was nice.

On every insertion was an accompanying gunship, which was a similar chopper but it never carried passengers or landed at the LZ. Its job was to circle overhead. It held the firepower of the two gunners and rocket pods on each side to provide some protection, if needed.

The rule was this: the team leader always had the final say on any decision to abort. Upon approach to the landing zone, if enemy fire started, it was an easy decision. And, sometimes, the clearing wasn't sufficient to land safely and the alternate LZ would have to be used.

The chopper usually never actually landed before we piled out. Recon team members went in a pre-arranged direction to the woodline and got out of sight. The chopper then left the LZ and I called him off when we were secure. Of course, we wanted those guys gone; any NVA in the area would know that there was enemy afoot and they would come right after us.

We walked in about 50 yards and re-grouped in a tight circle for about an hour and listened. If all was quiet, we compared maps and compass readings and began our mission.

We got used to each other after two or three missions and learned how to work together every minute. We learned to trust each other.

Bart was good, damned good. The first time he held his fist up, we froze, as practiced. Another hand signal a few seconds later and we did what we practiced in drills. Two guys on one side, three on the other side and flat down with rifles pointed toward the trail.

Sure enough, we heard the voices and then saw them in single file walking down the trail without a worry in the world. Their uniforms were well worn. All twelve of them had packs on their backs and were holding AK-47 rifles over their shoulders.

As they walked past us and out of sight, it occurred to me that we were in their backyard, this was their country, not ours.

That was the very first time I saw the enemy. All the mandatory yelling in boot camp every time we jabbed a bayonet into a hay bale, "Kill V.C., Kill V.C.", seemed so long ago. The soldiers in front of me were real. They were in uniforms, their faces were as dirty as their uniforms. They looked like they meant business. I felt so vulnerable. My heart seemed to race out of control. I could hardly think. Do we shoot? Will they see us? What do I do? All the preparation and training didn't calm me at that moment. As they passed by and away, the jungle returned to its stillness. My pounding heart left me feeling weak and I was soaked in sweat. So, I thought, that is the enemy, the famous NVA in person. They, who are claimed to fight to the death, mutilate and destroy Americans with hateful vengeance.

We didn't move for another hour. Checking our maps, we split from the trail and used the waterway. Walking on a gook trail is not advisable. We all hated the water, it was slow-moving and horrid, but quiet and not quite so dangerous as the trail.

The first time I crouched down under a spider hanging from a branch over the water, I thought I'd puke. That sucker was as big as a tennis ball with hair and long legs. I prayed my pack would not snag him. We were always on the lookout for snakes but when we got out of the water, I got my biggest surprise. Leeches. We all had leeches attached to us.

Each of us carried a small plastic bottle of scentless bug juice and now I knew why. One little drop of that stuff and the leech would fall off, leaving a bloody welt on the skin. One by one we dropped our trousers and helped each other get them off our backs and butts. Of course, we all checked ourselves at that very important spot below the belly.

Moving in water was a pain but sometimes the topography or vegetation required it. We were headed in the opposite direction as the gooks that passed us. Now, we had to find out if they were coming from a bunker complex in our assigned area.

We didn't find a thing for the next three days and when I heard the chopper coming after us, my heart sang. I switched frequencies, made contact with the pilot and waited. When the chopper was about 500 yards out, we popped a smoke, a beer can sized metal cannister with a pin and spoon similar to a grenade. When thrown out into the opening, the pilot knew exactly where to go and the shifting of the very thick, colored smoke helped him determine wind direction for landing.

What an exhilarating feeling to be in the air and safe. Maybe the best part was the air blowing in our faces. It was so cool, literally.

More hot days followed. More sandbags were filled. The sound of hammering and sawing was unmistakable and close. We had been told that more hooches were coming. Hooches were small plywood living quarters with galvanized metal roofing. Each rectangle was one room with studded walls, plywood floor and a plywood door at each end. Sawed openings on each door were covered with metal screening. The floor was off the ground with one or two steps from the ground up to the door. Our Civil War cots would be lined up with three on each side so we'd each have a little area. We all scrounged wooden ammo boxes to keep our soap, writing stuff and any other personal items. Up until now, the only teams that had hooches were those that captured a prisoner. The scarcity of plywood prevented more building for awhile but the plywood began to roll in.

I had two big events happen on the same day. First, my beady-eyed office buddy stopped by long enough to tell me the first sergeant wanted to see me. I had been meritoriously promoted to lance corporal. Whoopty-do.

Secondly, my mom sent a package. I had two cans of my favorite boned chicken, two half-melted Milky Ways, two pair of white underwear. No one in Recon wore underwear. What would be the point in that environment? And, two more goodies: a nice letter from my mom and dad and the handball gloves I asked them to get for me. All the guys wore them. We cut off the gloves' fingers to the first knuckle. They fit tightly and protected our hands in the jungle, especially in the Highlands when we had to go through long stretches of 20-foot high elephant grass with razor sharp edges.

I learned that lance corporals were not exempt from burning

shitters. It was the worst job of all. Our latrines were three holes inside a stinky, hot, little plywood shed on runners. Under the three well-used holes sawed out of plywood were three 50-gallon drums with metal handles. The drums were cut in half. It was a two-man work party. We were given work gloves and a five gallon can of diesel fuel. Our mission was to burn the crap out of the barrels, literally. Reaching under carefully, we grabbed the handles and dragged out the first drum a few feet. The same process was used on the middle one. It was placed next to the first and a few inches apart. Now was the hard part. We had to hoist the third drum to the top to form a pyramid. We poured the five gallons of diesel fuel into the three half barrels and lit a cigarette. We tossed the lit butts into the two bottom barrels, yelled "fire in the hole," grabbed the empty fuel can and walked away. Thick black smoke billowed into the air like a roaring inferno. We put the charred barrels back under the three-holer a while later.

I got back to the 3-C-2 tent to greet little beady-eyes who was handing out our monthly malaria pill. I needed more salt tablets, too. I had to take two huge tablets per day because I perspired so much. I just washed them down with a slug of iodine-laced water. There was no water to be found that one could drink without a dose of iodine. It took getting used to and to this day, when I smell iodine, it brings back memories of our drinking water in Viet Nam.

CHAPTER 6

During my eleven months in Recon, I was credited with 14 long-range missions. My first long-range mission was far from our base camp in Quang Tri. We were inserted by helicopter about a day's walk from the Ho Chi Minh trail, close to Laos. We were way out of radio range and there would be no fixed-wing support of rockets, bombs and napalm to help us if we got in the shit, as they said in Recon. We were totally on our own with a pretty good chance of never being heard from again. That is not an exaggeration.

Our mission would consist of a drop in an LZ and we would make our way to a predesignated spot on the famous trail from North Viet Nam where the NVA were spotted from air surveillance as having major stockpiling of troops, supplies and food. The trail accommodated trucks and they had their own hidden fortresses. Our job was to find them, stay well-hidden from their patrols and observe them with binoculars and take notes of what we observed.

After about two days of observing, we then had to rendezvous with a chopper at a given time and place for extraction. We had better be there. The chopper, with limited fuel, couldn't very well go looking for us. We always had the choice to bunk my radio on the insertion or keep it with me. We all agreed that I should keep it in my pack even though the extra weight could be a burden if we had to move fast. If we were being pursued, if we had wounded or if we had to change our plans to meet at a small opening or somewhere, I wanted that radio with me to direct the chopper. Otherwise, Walter Cronkite's daily body count would have five more to add.

So, we packed our gear, studied the maps and discussed the what if's and fiddled with the compasses to preset azimuths. Part of the routine was almost always writing a letter home. I never, not once, wrote of dangerous missions or firefights. But, on the other hand, I tried not to make it sound too boring or they would be suspicious of what I was leaving out. My parents, too, had a little plan, I suspected. They never said anything about politics, body count news, protests and all the other stuff going on at home. At that time, we just didn't know much. Sure, there was some scuttlebutt about all that but it was pretty sketchy and unclear.

About our only link to the "world," as we called the U.S. and home, was an old edition of *Stars and Stripes*. But, they only printed the good stuff and not real news. I first learned of an American astronaut landing on the moon from a front-page picture of the moon and the large, lettered headline, "U.S. Lands First Man on the Moon." Wow! What news! At the time we saw the paper, we were at the ammo dump picking out grenades and smoke to go out on a mission. The paper was on an old beat-up wooden chair right next to the door of the shack.

The ammo dump had a small shack that was cobbled together by debris from somewhere. An old salty Marine sergeant lived there and ran the place. No one ever went inside. I tried not to even look him in the eyes. He was crazy, I mean really, really looney. He almost always had a snake nailed up next to the door. He cooked them all the time. I never saw him at the mess tent. He looked like he would have been in his prime towards the end of WWI. What a character.

With letters written, our little area tidied up, we hiked up past the office to post our letters and five ready-for-the-jungle Recon Marines headed to the chopper pad and ammo dump. It was 0730 hours and already sweltering; my greasy camo paint on my arms and face was getting a little runny from the heat already and I could feel my back was wet from being against my pack.

It was a long ride to the Laotian border. Christ, I didn't want to be there.

One quick circle over the LZ and the chopper made a sharp bank and dove for the ground. It came up fast and we hit the ground at a fast pace to the tree line. The chopper took off right away and rather than circle once to wait for me to call in, he made a beeline away. I gave him the all clear and turned off my radio to save the battery. There wasn't a use for it for the next five days. The going was slow, hot and tiring, the terrain mountainous. By nightfall, we should have been closer, but we were forced to stop for the night. We knew we must be within range of their night patrols.

NVA patrols consisted of eight to ten soldiers. They were quiet, tactical and mean as hell. We were, as always, vigilant and without the relay station hourly reports. Our wrist watches would do just fine.

It must have been about mid-morning when we could see what looked like a lot of daylight through the jungle canopy. We thought that there must be a large opening ahead. And then we thought we heard a truck. We were there. We were not only there, we were too close.

We changed direction because it was getting too open and we slowly headed for the thick tangle of vines and cover. Oh, how I hated those spots. It was good protection from being seen but we had to share our hideouts with spiders, centipedes, biting ants and other godawful creatures. But it was a very, very good spot to hang out for a couple of days.

The first notation in the little notebook that John carried was the precise time it took to get from the LZ to this spot. The compasses were reset for our return journey. There would probably be no overnight on the way back unless we were being followed. In that case, we would have had to make a diversion so they wouldn't know our destination.

This time, we removed our packs and arranged them next to us so, if need be, we could be one with the ground to avoid detection. Settling in, we began our job. Holy smokes, what a setup they had. There were people milling around, others unloading a truck filled with ammo boxes. There were dark green tarps with big bags of rice underneath. Under the jungle canopy, there were tents hidden from view from above. It was like a miniature city. And then I noticed the sentries all around.

Our notetaking began and we took turns with the binoculars and whispered what we saw. The binoculars were old and beat-up. I imagined Patton looking through them at Rommel's tanks.

We were careful to keep them as low to the ground as we could, hoping there would not be a visible glare off the lenses.

After an hour or so of getting the layout down and sketching it with notes, we all looked at the maps together and planned. If we were spotted and had to evacuate fast, this is where we would go if we could. If we had to split up, meet here. We decided when we would have to leave to rendezvous. I was hungry, tired, scared shitless and I couldn't stop every large Laotian mosquito from biting me.

Their night patrols began to gather. Eight NVA started across the opening with their AK-47s locked and loaded. It was very unlikely that they would have found us but, damn, they were coming right at us. We were about 200 feet from a trail and they turned slightly towards that trail and disappeared. We had taken the time to construct a natural looking tangle to our rear, as well, to hide us better. If we needed to blast out, we could have done so easily. We saw the patrol return across the field five hours later and made a note of it.

The next day was interesting. The honcho in charge of our NVA friends kept everyone busy. Five trucks came in, all by one hour after daylight, and four trucks left after dark. They were spaced out about 20 minutes apart. They all had headlights with only slits on the lamp, just enough to see. We kept a running head count, weapons, stockpiling and the logistics of what was being offloaded and what was moving on. The troops were moving through with the outgoing trucks at night. Their uniforms looked newer and they sure looked young.

So, after two and a half days, we decided we had all the scoop we were going to get. It was time to split the scene. It gave us plenty of time to travel back to the LZ. After the night patrol passed us, we saddled up, sat back to back in our circle and took turns resting. At about 0500 hours, they again went across the field. We knew another patrol would not go out until after their morning chow, so we stood up, gave them the one finger salute and disappeared into the jungle, the quiet, moonlit jungle.

We moved slowly and stayed off the trails, referring to the compass and map frequently. And then, after taking breaks and readings, like magic, the beautiful opening lay ahead. We stayed well back into the deep shadows and sat down to listen. We couldn't see much with the binoculars but we were patient. We were afraid of having the chopper sighted and an ambush waiting.

It was a small, non-descript opening so we advanced toward it the next morning. We were three hours ahead of schedule but if there was anyone waiting for us, we'd better find out now. We got close enough to the opening to be able to throw a smoke cannister into it. Then, we waited. Bart heard it first. The whap-whap-whap of the rotor blades sounded like angels playing a harp. I spoke into the handset and corrected his course and said we would pop a yellow smoke. His final descent was a sight to behold and we split up and advanced to the opening. He landed and we jumped on that beautiful bird and flew off. Oh, what a feeling. I began to relax for the first moment in days. God, how I hated those missions.

I recall the difference in how I felt when I heard a helicopter because it depended on when I heard it. On the chopper pad in Quang Tri, when we heard the chopper coming in to get us, I had a terrible gut-wrenching feeling. It was awful. But, at the end of a mission when I first heard that same sound as it was coming in to extract us from the jungle's grip, it was an exhilarating feeling of joy and relief. Oh, the breeze felt so good as we circled above the LZ once and buzzed off toward "home."

Our long ride with the whapping of the rotor blades made me sleepy. I was just starting to relax and doze off when a turn and steep bank to approach Quang Tri brought me alert once again. We got off the chopper, gave the crew a thumbs up and gave the pilot a sharp salute. I think he must have been glad that he hadn't been with us. Everybody's gotta be somewhere, I guess. We didn't get to pick where.

Well, I'll be, yahoo! Looky that. Upon arrival at the head of the Charlie Company road was a line of brand spankin' new hooches all lined up in a straight row. Making our way down the line to 3-C-2, we waved to some of the guys and chatted for a bit about "the Trail."

Two steps up, open the door and inside. All our gear was in disarray and towards the center. That's all right. I knew my ragged old cot. There was an irregularly shaped dark stain near the upper edge. I figured it was a blood stain. And, from the location, it would have been an upper torso wound. Further deduction would lead me to believe that the poor old rickety thing must surely be Civil War era, as I have already stated. I could only wonder if the young fella was an enlisted man or some famous general. I could picture the surgeon sawing off his arm as he lay there on my cot.

John and Bart came back from G-2 which was quite pleased with our work. That night, as I stretched out on my Civil War cot, it occurred to me that 500-pound bombs were probably already dropped from a B-52 using the coordinates we provided G-2. Body count.

CHAPTER 7

I'd been there in the land that they called Viet Nam for one month. My buddies and I bonded, we trusted each other and were a real team. We had all the C-rations we wanted, there were plenty of powdered eggs, milk and potatoes. I wondered how they turned milk into a powder? My guess was that it was not milk. We had iodine for the water, they gave us malaria pills to keep us healthy and our own rifle to protect us in case there's a fight. Not bad. I should have been more grateful I suppose.

After our shower at the local spa, we were told to saddle up for 0700 hours tomorrow. I was told to report to the Comm shack ASAP to get wire, 2-PRC-25s, whip antenna with base and a case of batteries. The next day we were going to the "Rock Pile."

Aptly named, the Rock Pile was a mountain of sheer cliffs of slag stone and boulders put there by God himself in a humorous contrast to the surrounding boredom. The purpose for our little romantic getaway was to relieve another team that had been there for a couple of weeks. The Rock Pile was called Sierra Relay.

We would be the team responsible for communicating with however many teams were out on missions within our sector. There were typically only one or two teams, but sometimes three. We had radio watch 24 hours per day on rotation.

With all our gear loaded into a CH-46 Stallion chopper, we headed for Sierra. This was my first ride in a CH-46, a large two-rotor helicopter with a hydraulic tailgate. There were three portal windows on each side and in the States there would be two rows of seats, one on each side. But, in our neck of the woods, we were pretty tough on equipment, so all the glass in the windows and the seats were removed. There was a pilot and co-pilot, crew chief and two gunners. If we were going on a mission, each team member would take a window to shoot out of if need be. As the months progressed, I would discover how handy those windows were for shooting and I remember the thud-thud-thud as the NVA bullets hit the chopper body. The CH-46 had an open door next to one of the gunners. It was a much faster exit from the cumbersome tailgate lift.

In this case, the Rock Pile was secure. The top of the pinnacle was only about 100 feet around. There was the standard metal landing pad laid on top. In a large rock crevasse, there was an opening for 3-4 people to sit. There were boards over the top and then green plastic and more boards. It kept everything dry but the heat inside was almost unbearable.

Radio watches were four hours with two men per watch. There was no check-in desk to confirm our reservations, so we had to make do with what we had. There were some boards scattered about and I'm glad we brought extra plastic ponchos. I cobbled together a little two-man collapsible lean-to arrangement. My old Scoutmaster, Doug Cranson, probably wouldn't have given me a merit badge for the effort. It was collapsible because it was on the edge of the landing pad. When a chopper came in, it had to be collapsed and boards thrown on the whole mess to keep it from turning into a sailboat. My roommate was Gary Hardy. He was kind of a floater and was assigned to us for this little ten-day camp-out.

Nick brought along a softball-sized ball of C-4, which was the explosive grayish putty-like material that was packed in the claymore mines used on missions. On every mission, we took two claymores. At night we sometimes put them out. They were made with curved plastic cases packed with C-4 and about 200 ball bearings. The fuse was set into the unit with a thin cord of about 20-25 feet. At the end was a little squeeze handle with lock. The idea was to put one or two out at night, strategically placed. If our friendly NVA wanted to sneak up on us, we would squeeze the handle, the mine would explode and all the gooks around would be sent to hell piecemeal. In all my time there, we set them out many times but never used them.

The C-4 made a very good fire that burned hot and fast. Without the fuse, there was no explosive concern. Some guys liked to pretend to warm up their C-rations with the stuff. Ham and lima beans, spaghetti, lard and meatballs and franks and beans were slightly less disgusting when warm if you really used an imagination. I didn't eat the crap, cold or warm.

What a dump the side of that cliff was. The drop-off was less severe than a sheer smooth cliff. It had mostly rubble that could be climbed but very, very unlikely to happen. We didn't even have a night guard out. There were mines put over the sides that would help, too.

In order to take care of one's bodily function needs, you had to carefully climb down about 15 feet to a little level area that someone made. Emphasize little. Then one must drop drawers and carefully sit on an ammo box so that you didn't get too far back; too far forward would not be good, either. When the ammo box teetered a little, it was just right. I always hoped, every time I climbed down there, that if a sniper got me, please, oh please, don't let me fall back into that shithole.

The first night on the Rock Pile, I learned it would be noisy all night. There were rats, great big New York City rats, everywhere. Rats went where the food was. That's why we were told not to eat in the Comm bunker. Gary and I had a couple of open C-rats that had cigarettes, crackers and chocolate. We couldn't sleep. The rats were literally walking on us. It was dangerous, too. You do not want to be bitten by a rat. Who knows when they could get a chopper in to get you. Rabies shots had to be started very soon. The next morning, we moved our house and put no food inside. That was Christmas Day. There was no white Christmas 1968 for us. The temperature was mid-90s and we were socked in most of the time.

Without warning, we heard a small plane approaching. It circled around us twice before someone came out of the bunker and yelled that it was making the rounds and dropping a Red Cross package. It was a dual propeller Bronco spotter plane. All of a sudden, out from the side tumbled a cardboard box end over teakettle towards us. It missed the top and crashed into the rocks below.

It seemed too far to retrieve. But crazy Bart said, "I'm going." He put on an empty pack and his handball gloves and down he went. It was an ill-advised adventure. We were quite concerned about his insistence to attempt retrieval of the Red Cross care package. The severity of the drop-off, with all the loose rocks, made it very dangerous to maneuver - never mind the mines and the rubbish thrown over the edge. But down and over he went, with all eyes on his every movement. He did well enough though and took his time. Stuff was scattered in all the crevices, but below our trash field.

After about half an hour, he found his way up and over the top.

He was soaked with sweat and panting. Someone got a poncho liner and spread it out. Bart dumped out the contents. It was actually pretty funny considering the effort and danger he went through. There were about a dozen small combs, several small tubes of toothpaste, three or four toothbrushes, six to eight Christmas cards from the fifth grade class of a school in Texas, one and a half pair of white tube socks, two used paperback books which we all took turns reading, five rosary beads and a ruptured plastic bottle of baby powder.

Everyone fought over the powder and I told Bart I was holding out for the two turtle doves. He took all the ribbing in stride.

I took one string of the rosary beads, sat down, held it tight and thought of home. It seemed so far away and only a memory that could never be relived. At that moment I felt so alone and sorry for myself. I tried to hide it.

We had a 50-gallon drum of water that we tried to keep in the shade but it was putrid iodine water that couldn't quench a thirst. We had to ration our supply. Which was worse, I wondered, out on a mission with death at every turn of the trail or this rat-infested prison where you can't even take a shit without fear of falling back into it or being the target of sniper practice. I didn't even have a coin to flip.

The days went by slowly. I ran new wire, set up the new antenna and was on the last battery for the radio when we heard the chopper coming in. Our lean-to was already dismembered, my gear on my back and out we went. Good-bye.

We hit the spa first. The Quang Tri River water was less filthy than we were, so the shower felt good. It was almost time for evening chow so I put on my cleanest dirty clothes. I was soaked with sweat already.

Clean clothes. I must explain. There was a mama-san who came around once in a while to collect our dirty clothes. She had a clever way of keeping track of what belonged to whom, or so I thought. If you were there when she came around, she would take your stuff and put it in one of our large, nylon mail sacks and she would wander away and come back two to three days later with what seemed to us to be nice clean clothes. By clothes, I mean shirts, trousers, socks, USMC boxer shorts and t-shirts. The boxers and tees were for around the hooch on free time, not to wear on a mission.

When mama-san collected clothes, she expected payment. Whatever U.S. currency we had needed to be exchanged at the office for MPC, which was a made-up currency. MPC is Military Payment Currency. We all called it funny money. Every so often, they would change the design and we would have to exchange it or lose it. I didn't need much because there was nothing much to buy.

So anyway, mama-san came with my clean clothes and they were nice to wear around base camp. One day, we got permission to go down to the Quang Tri River for a swim. We brought our rifles. It was a hot, hot day. The area was essentially secure but we knew enough to never go anywhere outside of camp without rifle and ammo. So, down by the river we saw a bunch of women all chewing their favorite beetlenut. It was like a nutty narcotic gum. Those who had teeth chewed it all the time. The women were split into groups. Some had a mountain of GI clothes at water's edge, scrubbing; another group carried them up to a line of fires with a pole three to four feet above with GI clothes hanging above the fire to dry. Another group removed the clothes from above the fire to place on sheets of GI plywood to press with a heavy, hot iron. The most interesting part of the whole operation was the fire. We learned that the villagers couldn't use wood because of a general lack of trees. They were predominately rice farmers. The most valued possession they owned was a water buffalo. Their fuel supply was dried water buffalo dung. It was like cow flops. Gee, I thought our clothes smelled just fine. A few months later, I mailed a box home of some minor souvenirs I had picked up. I also sent home a pair of camo shirts and trousers I wore a few times on missions. I heard they were hard to get stateside so I mailed some home. I got a letter some weeks later and my mom was inquiring about the box I sent home. It remained unopened and she wondered if she should open it because something inside must have spoiled. It occurred to me that I should pass on to her my permission to remove the clothes for a good laundering. Maybe we had just gotten used to the smell.

We all had a good swim in the river with no leeches. A few weeks later, our beady-eyed friend, the Company clerk, who was now a corporal, came by looking for three volunteers to go to the Philippines for two weeks to be qualified hard hat divers. It wasn't like Navy master divers. I understood that it was a simple qualification to dive 100-150 feet to learn about compressed air and equipment and the like. It was the first step to go into Force Recon. Recon was the elite special forces of the Marine Corps and Force Recon was the elite of Recon and the pinnacle of the Marines' elite fighting force. Of course, I wanted to do it. I had already talked about the other qualification with the First Sergeant, which was to be jump qualified. I wanted my wings and now was my chance for deep sea diving. Five of us were chosen with one officer, a second lieutenant named John Shinault. He was a nice, down to earth guy and we all got along with him well. He went out on missions with Charlie Company teams. In order for him to be promoted to first lieutenant, he needed to have so many missions with Recon under his belt. So, the five of us had to go down to the river every day and practice life-saving stuff, hard swimming and general goof-off. In just a few days we would fly out of Da Nang for the Philippines.

I never made it. The First Sergeant called us in to say sorry but we're short-handed and we were told to go out to look for a bunker complex the next day. Crap!

We did go out and on the second day we found the bunkers that the gooks made for shelter, safety and a medical unit for their wounded. It was near good water and not far from where our grunts (infantry) kicked ass a few weeks prior. Recon had the nickname "super-grunts." We found the openings to the two bunkers, along with bamboo poles and woven branches to provide shade cover outside for eating and to hide the openings.

It was late afternoon so we did our nightly routine and didn't get too close to compromise ourselves. By first light it seemed obvious that the place was abandoned. Bart and Juan snuck in and up to the openings. We all followed and checked out the area. Nothing.

"Chu-hoi, chu-hoi," we shouted, which means surrender. Nothing.

Then, on the count of three, a couple of us pulled the pin on a grenade and chucked them in each bunker. We stepped back and out of the way to a thundering explosion. Nothing. We saw no need to go in. We found what our mission called for and going in could be big trouble. I've gone in a couple and it is horrible. They're dark and gooks booby-trapped their abandoned tunnels and bunkers. They knew how to undo their traps but GI's didn't. Inside were spider holes, which were little holes with branches covered with dirt. In the hole could be punji stakes, sharpened and tipped with poison or human excrement.

Or, they could put a snake in the hole or a trip wire with explosives. They had all sorts of little surprises. Hence, the grenade toss.

The next logical move for us was to beat feet fast and sure in the direction of the LZ for pick-up the next day. After a while, it was time to settle in at a big thicket and just wait a couple of hours and just listen. If there were any gooks within hearing distance of the grenades, they would investigate. We did not want to meet them halfway. Nothing. They had moved on and the whole mission was a success and we were all alive for yet another day.

CHAPTER 8

It was good to be back to our cozy and mostly safe base camp. Ol'
Sarge, at the ammo dump, had two snakes nailed up next to his shack
door. After I unloaded smoke, grenades and some M-79 rounds, I
asked the ol' buzzard where he got them.

"Where do you think?" he said. "Where would you be if you were
a snake?"

"Gee, I guess I hadn't thought much about it," I answered.

"Exactly," he emphasized, "That's why I'm having snake for
supper and you ain't."

I figured that answer was as close to knowing as I would ever get,
so I started to amble away. He stopped us all in our tracks.

"You're walkin' on 'em, assholes," he barked with pride.

Nick said, "You say what?"

"I said, you're walkin' on 'em," he said. "Snakes are smart," he
added. "They know where to go to get food, stay safe and cool. Dem
snakes are all over this whole place under all this steel. At night, when
it cools off, dem dare snakes come out on top. I go out and shoot what
I want."

Since I foolishly brought up the subject, I went for it. "So, Sarge,
how come we never hear any shootin' here at night? You'd never get
away with it."

"I got a little 22 and mounted a flashlight. Now don't get any ideas,
Mr. Recon asshole. Deez are my snakes so stay the hell out."

"I promise, Sarge. I was just asking."

Our feet were killing us, they felt raw. We were in water and mud for the best part of six days. I knew my feet needed salve. So straight to the aid station we went. The corporal had us remove our boots and had us soak our feet with socks on in this liquid. It felt like putting my feet on a hot grill but settled down after a couple of minutes. Then, he slowly removed a couple of our socks and wrinkled white skin came off with the socks. We got the idea and finished our own. Then back in the solution of salt, battery acid and bleach went the feet, or so it seemed. We all got a little tube of tassum to put on our feet with instructions to keep our feet up and open to the air. Sure, doc, no sweat. Our maid was scheduled for the next day anyway and little beady eyes would, I'm sure, make a chow run for us. We'd just relax with our feet up. He even gave us a new pair of pretty olive drab, USMC issued socks.

We hobbled back to 3-C-2 to a big surprise. We had company. The sixth cot in our little hooch was taken. A Navy corpsman sat in a chair he scrounged somewhere, reading a Playboy magazine. John asked him if he just stopped by to take out a book or what? Rod McKeon said he was temporarily assigned to us for two months. I heard somewhere that Navy corpsman were assigned on a volunteer basis to some Recon teams. That's cool. We were lucky to have him. We would all get acquainted after our much-anticipated shower. We limped back to 3-C-2 in our skivvies and truck-tire flip flops. "Just in time to tend to our feet, doc," said Bart.

"Did you get some salve?" Doc asked. "Yah, sure. It feels pretty good, too," Nick chimed in. We all had our feet up. There were enough lawn chairs and wooden chairs to go around.

"That salve is good stuff. My feet feel better already," I added. Doc told us that the salve we had was used for everything - burns, rashes, VD, immersion feet and small wounds. I looked forward to having Doc with us. He could come in as handy as pockets on a shirt.

So we gave him the whole rundown of what he needed to know to go out with the boys. It seemed like he was looking forward to it. Maybe he was nuts. Two days later, our favorite corporal came down with the news to go to G-2. We were going out. My poor feet.

As it turned out, we thought our first sergeant was looking after us. He knew we needed a couple more days to let our feet dry out. We got a very special assignment. It was called an unofficial in-country R&R (rest and recoupment). Man-o-man!

Apparently Cua Viet Airbase, which was right on the South China Sea, was getting harassing mortar fire at night from some VC. We were to be sent down to end it. Our mission was to run night ambush patrols along the beach and try to stamp out the little buggers. Good deal. We could sleep by day and ambush VC at night. It couldn't get better than that. Little did we know, it would get even better than we had imagined.

With our feet bandaged and gear ready, including truck-tire flip flops, I didn't have time to ask my mom to send a beach umbrella and lotion. I guess I could use my new salve. Our chopper ride was exhilarating. Hi ho, hi ho, it's off to the beach we go.

It was gorgeous, a balmy 105 degrees with a salty sea breeze and real waves. The sand was pure white and not a stone to be found. Our destination seemed more like an outpost than a base camp. We were on the west side of the Cua Viet River, its mouth, and it was very wide with swift-moving brown water. Rather than say it was fresh water, we called it not salt water.

On the east side of the river was the Air Force base, a sprawling thing with a large airfield, buildings and barracks to support a large unit. Our little outpost was like F-Troop. We checked into this little hooch only to discover that our little beady-eyed company clerk corporal had a brother, or it looked like it. He looked puzzled at our arrival and called for the captain, a skinny little guy who said two or three times that he was in charge. He briefed us on the unacceptable conditions caused by the nightly mortar attacks. We had to do something. We asked for maps and compasses and other stuff we could think of that they wouldn't have. It's a good thing we brought ammo for our rifles. He asked what we needed grenades for - they didn't come that close. Yo-boy!

So, what we did get were two-man pup tents, top and bottom white union suits, entrenching tools and a direct order to stop the mortar harassment in two days. Our real orders were for four days.

We were introduced to a Navy lieutenant whose pimply face put him at about sixteen years old, but he must have been older. We were commanded to report our whereabouts at all times because he was a forward observer off the *U.S.S. Enterprise* and he would be conducting maneuvers to destroy a force of enemy VC and he didn't know why we were there but we must stay out of the way and check in with him at all times. Yes, sir!

We pitched our little olive drab canvas tents. Then we stripped down. We forgot our swimsuits and beach towels, so six naked Recon guys trudged through the sand with our truck-tire flip flops to protect our feet. The sand was burning hot. I had brought a PRC-25 radio and two batteries. I carried it in my back pack. I always had to have a pack.

I set the frequency to what the Admiral gave me and called him to get a radio check. He was furious. "You didn't sign out, where are you?" I told him to step outside and look towards the ocean, I would wave to him. He was not amused. We swam and waded and talked until evening chow and went back to get our C-rations. Pimply face was so mad he wanted to withhold our C-rations. That didn't work for him.

Just before dark, we dressed in our white union suits and boots. I, of course, stuck out like a sore thumb with my USMC issue olive drab canvas backpack and radio. Our two e-tools were put in my pack. We conferred over the map and made plans. The Admiral didn't know that G-2 gave us our own maps and we had our compasses. That dumb ass.

Off we went about two hundred yards and parallel to the shore. At night, the moon reflected the white sand and we really did provide quite a contrast. The white sand extended inland from the shore only about fifty yards and turned into a dry brown soil with a sort of beach grass and large hummocks of sandy soil, not unlike high dunes.

Reports of mortar fire were estimated to come from much further inland and further away from the river. We felt pretty safe. We dug a sort of foxhole for some protection just in case and stretched out. The digging was easy so we made it a little bit big to relax. With two guys on watch, four of us could be still and listen to the waves. The sky was a spectacular Milky Way. I thought it was pretty amazing that between us, we knew a lot of formations. It was fun to have everyone point out the Seven Sisters, the bears and the ones we made up.

"Where?" Nick asked when I pointed out the Vulvias Extrudis. "I don't see it, what's it look like?"

We all got a pretty good chuckle.

Just up from the high tide mark was great, it was so cool and refreshing and the breeze kept away the mosquitoes and bugs that would normally torture us all night. The hours between 2400 and 0400 were the best.

On watch and awake, the moon and stars brought the desire to be home. How could you not think of home? Heck, even in the jungle, leaning against each other in a circle, you couldn't help but beam yourself home. I remembered the times in Boy Scouts lying in Whitney's hayfield listening to the scoutmaster and looked where he pointed out the Big Dipper and followed the line to the North Star.

"Use the stars to navigate at night," he told us.

I never thought about Viet Nam back then when I was in scouts. I couldn't find it on the map if you gave me three bags of M&Ms. But there I was, not quite grasping the purpose and gravity of it all. We knew nothing at all about the politics and world news or the protesting or the building hatred for us guys who were placed here like chess pieces to be moved around and around but really going nowhere.

An hour before dawn we filled the hole in the sand and headed back to the fort. We all crashed without chow. Just before noon we were startled awake by a thunderous crash of an explosion. Our forward observer friend was conducting maneuvers with the Enterprise, thinking he would pick some likely spots the VC would be and call in a fire mission. He used the wrong coordinates and nearly killed us all. It was far enough away to be harmless to us but it sure was loud. He really got chewed out for that blunder.

We were in for a treat. We had an amtrack cross the river to deliver food, mail and other supplies. An amtrack is like a large tank, but amphibious.

We were invited to go across the river to the flyboys' base. We jumped at the chance. All dressed up in our not so clean and wrinkly olive drabs, we climbed up the amtrack and hung on. Once we hit the water, I thought we'd sink for sure but that diesel engine, the size of a locomotive, chugged away.

The base was a marvel; we were like kids at Disney for the first time. Everyone eyed us with disdain and I didn't blame them. We were hungry so we asked where the mess hall was. Without saying anything to us or getting too close, the guy in a neatly starched and pressed uniform pointed to a building with a little sign that said "Sea Breeze Club." Okay, Joe, worked for me.

Holy smokes, it was a real club. It had air conditioning, a beautiful bar with beer taps, lounge tables and chairs, carpeting and gorgeous waitresses with round eyes. We sat at a nice large round table but the waitress kicked us out. We missed the little sign that said something about officers. We wanted to sit at the bar anyway. We took up the whole end of the bar. They even had menus. I ordered a cheeseburger club. It was hot and delicious with real meat. The French fries had real potato inside and a crispy outside. I ordered two beers but the bartender suggested just one at a time. He said something sarcastic about not running out. We lingered for a while and finished our third beer. That's where our luck ran out. We decided to split the bill six ways and we did. The bartender pointed to another little sign we had missed as well. They only accepted US currency. We didn't have any. We had to exchange all our cash for funny money (MPC) in Quang Tri. We told him what we were doing there and he seemed impressed and told us to just leave. All that chow and beer for free.

We found the PX (post exchange). They had all kinds of stuff. They had uniforms, food (real food), gadgets and other electronic stuff. We checked this time and, yes, they accepted MPC. We found out later that the Air Force hired a private company to run the club, hence the US currency only. I bought three packs of unfiltered Camels.

We had to catch the amtrack to cross the river at 1600 hours and we were almost late. With all the jostling around on that diesel behemoth, we all felt sick by the time we got to F-Troop. All that rich, spicy food and beer was giving us grief. Off to the latrine and then a nap before dark.

It was another quiet night in the dark. It was pitch black with heavy cloud cover. The VC weren't out again that night. A dense fog rolled in and the sound of the waves guided us back to the fort.

It was so hot that morning we couldn't sleep in that little pup tent so we fashioned together a little lean-to arrangement to block the sun and that worked pretty well.

For our last night's excursion, we decided to find the little guys, if they were out there. We followed our plan and slowly zig-zagged through the maze of dunes, tall grass and brush. About 0200 hours we thought we heard voices and then we were sure of it. Knowing it would be a two- or three-man VC mortar team, they would be mobile and would move out of the area quickly should they hear us.

We whispered out a decision. With our selectors on full automatic and Juan with a few M-79 cannisters at the ready, we lined up and let 'em have it. The firepower and noise were impressive, not to mention the element of surprise. We kept it up for two or three magazines each and Juan stepped out the M-79 a little on each shot.

We never considered pursuit. It was possible and maybe even likely that we got a lucky shot in there somehow. In their retreat, they would know that the Americans were on their case and would think twice about wandering out there in the semi-open terrain. We found our way back, satisfied that we fulfilled our orders. Our feet were pretty much back to normal. Pimples was called back to the Enterprise while we were at the club the day before. He never said good-bye. We met our chopper later for a ride to Quang Tri. We were rested and content. The first sergeant stopped by and liked our stories. It was a very pleasant visit. On his way out, he turned and in his best first sergeant deep voice, he looked at John and said, "Corporal, go to G-2 and get your orders, you're going out tomorrow." He turned and left.

CHAPTER 9

While I was packing, John and Bart returned from G-2 with orders for an area of surveillance near the Ho Chi Minh Trail, again. This time would be further north with the Trail separating us from the Laotian Mountains. Another long-range mission at hand. Doc seemed pleased and maybe a little excited. I reminded Doc that our scenic tour would be on the ground, not from the air. If we were compromised, it would be like slamming a stick through a hornet's nest. He packed in silence.

What made this mission a little different was that we were taking a sniper with us. We were not happy. Seven guys were a lot. John went to the first sergeant to complain and the old boy agreed. But, he told us that the sniper would go with us and the doc would not. Doc was pissed. I told Doc I would be willing to let him fill in for me. John just glared at me. Team leaders have no sense of humor.

Taking a sniper meant just one thing. We had a target that G-2 got wind of and wanted that target taken out. We were given a picture of what the uniform would probably look like. The sniper, who was a Recon guy from Delta Company, stopped by to go over a bunch of plans, back-up plans, what-ifs, and all that good stuff. At least he was one of ours.

The fact is, I requested sniper school after my third week at Quang Tri. Others had interest as well. I was a sharp shooter in boot camp and felt confident. We went to the rifle range, which was pretty basic but it was a place to practice with mortars, M-60 machine guns and the law (shoulder-mounted grenade launcher – very powerful). Anyway, I did my best shooting and was weeded out. Only two guys passed to go to sniper school. This guy with us had been around and went through extensive training stateside. I felt somewhat better but he still wouldn't have an M-16 for fire power if we needed it. As it turned out, he would have an M-16. His sniper rifle was dismantled and in his pack. Good deal. If he used the rifle to take out a general, it would be left behind, minus the bolt, which would be quickly removed and flung in the brush somewhere. A general was our target. We were told what to look for to identify where he would be.

It was another long chopper ride. Our chosen LZ was a very small opening that appeared on the map to be a tight fit for a chopper landing. We were prepared to rappel down a rope, which we've all practiced and didn't look forward to. Going down was okay but upon extraction we would have to all hang from the knotted rope while the chopper lifted off and took us over the tree tops to another place where he could land. It would have been a dangerous and terrifying ride. I tried not to think of it. We also examined the map for an alternative LZ. I wished that I could have had time to see the rope. How it was attached to the chopper "D" ring was pretty important. I remembered my Boy Scout knots.

The LZ was a secluded little opening of tall grass and brush and fairly open on three sides with a thicker tangle of brush on the south side. The chopper was about three feet off the ground when we dumped out, like usual. We didn't like the open terrain at all and went right for cover. The chopper took off right away and after a moment I conveyed all secure and the chopper and gunship disappeared. I turned off my radio. We checked our map and Bart led the way for a day's journey to the NVA and the famous Ho Chi Minh Trail. My stomach was tight, I was thirsty and I had to pee. At our first pause, we all peed, had a sip of water, marked the maps and continued.

Our instincts told us they wouldn't be looking for us. Those same instincts and the map told us we were close. It was getting late when we knew we were there. We heard no noise but we knew. John and Bart went ahead. They were gone for over half an hour before we spotted Bart to the north, further north than we expected. He signaled us and we made our way to him, then further to John, who was lying down and we did a sort of low crawl to him. Holy smokes. We were close, too close. It was a great hiding spot but too close. John and Bart whispered and Bart left us with slow meticulous movements. It would be dark soon and we were unsettled. After pitch black, Bart returned and we followed. We were going further north. Moving at night was a real trip. The air seemed to be quieter and ground litter could be noisy. But we got to our destination in another one hundred yards, further from the trail. There would be no pound cake tonight, just a couple of sips of water.

At first light, it was evident that Bart was on his game. Our view was decent and we were far enough away to observe their activity, be concealed and not worry about our slightest movement.

Man, what a layout. There were six large trucks, three or four fairly large camo tents, about a platoon of NVA, piles of supplies and a 10'x10' pile of neatly stacked ammo boxes six feet high. It was amazing. In addition to the platoon of NVA working around the area, there were people under the trucks and trees sleeping. We heard the trucks come in before daybreak. They travelled all night from depot to depot transporting troops and supplies south to amass a regiment or division of NVA with ammo and supplies to fight at their chosen locations.

We took turns eating in the morning and took notes all day. We didn't think about being so close to the NVA because we were distracted by all their activity. The more we observed, the more we learned. They had netting and branches over nearly everything, including the trucks.

In the afternoon, they put aside branches and uncovered dozens of gasoline cans. They filled up the trucks and began loading. With the binoculars, we could see clearly what the contents were. They stacked many boxes of large tins of what was probably food, boxes with large bags of rice, large cans that differed somewhat from the gas cans they used to fill the trucks. They were probably water cans. They mixed up the contents of every truck so each truck had some weaponry, ammo, food and miscellaneous gear. The troops would walk. We had heard that the trucks got stuck in mud a lot. The roads sometimes disappeared, sometimes from the B-52 bombs, and had to be rebuilt by the troops. The trucks could also be an easy target for the Phantom bomb runs and strafing. So, they moved at night and stayed concealed. That is why we were there. Our mission was to find them, observe activity, count everything and document exact coordinates. By the end of the second day our job was done.

There was one curious detail we discovered early in the day. The incoming trucks the last night carried six women in their black wardrobe. They looked dirty and haggard through the binoculars, as were the troops. They must have had a difficult journey. The women were fed as they squatted down together. Afterward they were herded into a tent and that's the last we saw of them except when they came out to squat and pee. The curious part was the activity around the tent. All day the men would go in and then come out again in a short while. So these six women were the comfort women we had heard about. Commandeered from the villages up north, the women were the travelling whores for the NVA. I felt bad for them. I wondered what would happen to these slaves. They would soon die, I was sure, like the NVA they were with. We wrote down the coordinates.

Decision time was upon us. To take the shot or not take the shot. The general was easily identified as he was the sole inhabitant of a modest tent and two armed NVA stood outside guarding the entryway.

The general went in and out several times a day to relieve himself and give orders. He always ate in the same spot, alone. Our sniper moved away from us for a couple of hours and he found a spot as far away as he could and still see the tent opening. He found a stick shaped like a sling shot for a rifle rest and made a comfortable place for a good shooting position and looked through the scope a long time. We could barely see him.

He slowly found his way back to us but left the Weatherby rifle with the 50-caliber bore in place. We had to decide. Luke, our sniper, wanted to go for it. John confirmed the decision was made. My stomach tightened again.

The timing was right and the plan seemed solid. The NVA had no patrols out. They didn't know the jungle area at all, their task at hand was to move supplies and troops down the Ho Chi Minh Trail.

Once the sniper took his shot, there would be mass confusion before they organized enough to form a patrol to come after us. What we didn't know was, how far would they come? Would they be relentless? Who was second in command? Would he sacrifice time and not get the convoy on the road when it got dark? We believed our sniper had the upper hand.

Our chopper would be there at 0700 hours the next morning. If he took his shot at their evening chow, we could have made it but with little time to dally. We would have been on the move all night, making slower progress, but the moon would have been out.

The general had a habit of getting out of his tent, pausing to stretch and putting his hands on his hips, looking around. That would be Luke's moment. The plan was for us to leave within the hour. That would be two hours before their evening chow. We weren't there long enough to see that pattern develop but it was close enough. We would have been gone for two or three hours before he took his shot. He would catch up to us and we'd be gone. It would be faster and quieter for him to travel alone. We had to remember that even though we were travelling away from the hornet's nest, there could be another ahead. We were further north than when we came in so our route would have been different and at night. We compared compasses and maps, checked our packs and rifles. We bid farewell to our new sniper friend and disappeared into the heart of darkness.

For the first couple of hours, Juan stayed with us. The moon wasn't nearly full but the light was good for us to travel. We were surprisingly quiet and our pace was faster than normal. Every fifteen minutes or so we stopped to listen and take a look at the compass. Bart had a star fix and a compass check was just a verification. And then, without being told, Juan dropped back a fair amount. We couldn't see him but we knew he was there. In another hour or so, Luke was expected to catch up. If he didn't show up, he would have missed us and we would have met up at the LZ.

We heard a noise like a bird. We froze and listened. In a few minutes, Juan came in with Luke who was winded and happy to see us. He said later that he loped along when he could and walked a quick step to catch up. He said no one was following. So far so good. We kept moving.

We missed the LZ by a little and would have gone by it if Nick hadn't seen it to our east. We were there. Were we there alone? We hid in the same thick crap where we started. It was 0530 hours. We had only an hour and a half to spare. I turned on my radio and we waited. It was quiet.

Then, movement to our left and noise. We were in the ready and knew what lay ahead for us. But then our worst fear was laid to rest; it was a wild boar or what looked like a boar that stepped into the open trees that we had stayed away from when we were inserted. We hadn't seen one of those critters before. Whew!

The chopper was a half hour late when we heard that beautiful noise. I called him in, threw a yellow smoke. He slipped right in with a gentle touch and lift-off.

Later, in the showers, Luke said he got the perfect shot right in the chest. With bullets the size of a small carrot, one didn't need to feel for a pulse; the general was dead. Luke said he even dismantled his Weatherby and slipped it in his pack.

"I wasn't about to leave that sweet thing," he said.

We complimented each other and he went back to Delta Company. Doc wanted to hear all about the whole mission. I think we all showed a little restraint because we didn't want to cross the line into nonchalance. We were good. We were tight. But life wasn't perfect; we didn't want to forget that.

CHAPTER 10

It was time to start my short-timers calendar. Our Company Clerk had a few blank copies and it seemed a little silly since I had months left to go on a thirteen-month tour of duty.

The short-timers calendar was a sort of distraction and at the same time a little pictorial representation for bragging rights. "Hey, Norm, how much time ya got left?" "285 days, why?" "I've got 42 and a wake-up - ha, ha." "Big fucking deal. Yippie for you."

The calendar was an outline of a woman with neatly drawn lines to create 395 boxes, numbered 1 through 395. Each numbered box would be colored in as each day passed by. Numbering would start at the woman's feet, go to arms, legs, torso and the real short-timers would end up coloring in the boxes on the breasts. Box #3 would be the left nipple, #2 the right, and the #1 would, of course, be the sweet spot and colored pink. There was always someone around with a box of crayons. It was a rather fun thing to do and compare. Guys like me kept our calendars with our writing gear out of sight. But guys with thirty days or less had theirs pinned to the wall front and center for all to see. The other calendar picture was an outline of Viet Nam. Going out on a mission meant catching up upon our return and making sure the calendar was correct. That was important stuff.

Receiving mail was a big deal and we all looked forward to a letter from home. Sometimes mail would get backed up and mail call would get big. Mom wrote the most and more often, while Dad added a little something at the end, but I know it was a struggle for him. But, he made an effort and I appreciated that. My dad wasn't much of a writer. As a matter of fact, he wasn't a very good communicator. He pretty much was a listener. And being a World War II vet, he had a better background of what I was probably going through. I believe in the old saying, "Still waters run deep." My younger brother and sister were pretty much into their own world at that time.

But Mom was mom. Her oldest was a Recon Marine in Viet Nam and that was the focal point of her life. She wrote a little about every day, almost like a diary and when she got three or four pages on her pretty stationery, she would put it in the mail. Of course, I would make my requests and she always accommodated me. For whatever reason, she sent me a can of boned chicken pieces that I devoured and then asked for every time I wrote home. She tried sending candy bars but that didn't work very well; it was a melted chocolate mess. Her chocolate chip cookies were good, a little dry and crumbled, but I got the idea.

Better than the taste were the memories. Eating the little pieces of cookie reminded me of when we were kids. The main part of our kitchen was a massive wood and porcelain cabinet (known as a "Hoosier Cabinet") with a pullout shelf to work on, a big flour bin, drawers and doors that held everything for the modern woman. Back in the '50s, I guess it was the cat's meow.

Every Saturday morning, Mom got the old washing machine hooked up to do the weekly wash, put it through the wringer, and then carry the basket of wet clothes out through the shed to hang out to dry on the clothesline. While waiting for the wash to dry, sometimes she would make chocolate chip cookies, and a big mixing bowl sat on the cabinet counter with lots of sumptuous cookie dough. We'd run in the back door through the kitchen and dip a finger in the bowl for a nice dollop of cookie dough, then away we would run, through the shed with the screen door slamming shut. Sometimes, we got away clean. And then there were the times we weren't quite so lucky and got a scolding. "If I don't have enough for another batch, you won't get any cookies," Mom would scold. It seems that the fear of getting caught never prevented another try, thinking that the next time we'd know where she was and evade capture. Moms all had four eyes and were always where you thought they weren't.

Sitting on a stack of sandbags, leaning against a plywood hooch and a half a world away from home, they were pleasant memories and yet sad. I grew melancholy when I received mail or a package from home, yet every day I craved more mail.

I thought I would get more mail from my friends at home but it was a rare day when I would get a letter from one of them. Like my brother and sister, I suppose they had their own lives.

I received mail once in a while from an aunt and an uncle. He had been in France and Germany during WWII and I presume he could relate to my situation. He sent me lots of jokes and cartoons and I really enjoyed them. He was also my godfather and our Catholic family was close. We all watched out for each other. Sundays meant church in the morning and visiting family in the afternoon. The men did all the daily chores, as they must, but they never made noise on Sunday, like mowing the lawn. Haying time was the big exception. When the hay was ready, it needed to be tended to, Sunday or not. Years after leaving the Marine Corps, I learned two big things: My mom said the rosary every night that I was in Viet Nam and she also saved every letter that I wrote her.

My letters home were rather generic. I consciously avoided writing too much detail of what Recon was or what we did. I tried to make it appear as boring as I could, playing up guard duty and filling sand bags. I may have forgotten to mention the Ho Chi Minh Trail, Laos, sniper team and other things like that. What would be the point? From time to time, I guess all of us sat on a pile of sand bags, dragged on a cigarette, and stared out into the nothingness. In some small way, it might have kept us all a little more grounded, maybe even sane. Recollections of childhood activities and the innocence of it all were the best.

I was only 20 years old but it seemed like a lifetime ago when I would go out behind the barn to the manure pile to dig worms for fishing down at the ravine. I'd take an empty pipe tobacco tin that Gramp saved for us kids, put a little dirt in and dig some worms. My old fishing pole took quite a beating but I caught my share of the little "six-inch native brookies." Yes, staring out into the vast blue universe was good tonic until it got just too hot to stand it. Then it was time for some iodine water, a salt tablet and back to Viet Nam. There would be no fishing that day.

We went on a couple of eventless missions with Doc tagging along. He was a natural. He knew his place and what to do and the added bonus was that he carried more medical supplies. I'm not sure if those supplies would ever help or not; if we got in the shit and if we were to break it off with one or two seriously wounded guys, it would be about four hours before we could get out. No matter what medicine is in the little green bag of tricks, four hours is a pretty long time to keep someone alive that is badly gunshot. No offense to Doc but having a priest who's a good shot would have been just as good.

One hot, humid Saturday we were all looking forward to evening chow. We had been extracted that morning from an exhausting trek in the jungle. It was three days of sweat and frustration. We had a grave registrar with us. I learned that a grave registrar is one who accompanies a team occasionally in search of the site of a downed plane or a missing Marine at the location of a battle. The registrar would help locate the missing person, mark the site, leave identification – like a dog tag – and take the other tag. We did our best to cover the remains for retrieval at another time. He carried an M-16 just like us but we knew he'd shoot himself or one of us if we were in a firefight. We wondered how that guy ever got through boot camp. He was a klutz and he couldn't be quiet even if his life depended on it – and it did. He carried an e-tool in his pack.

We were sent out to look for a pilot that was thought to have been shot down in a particular location. Two days before, there was a B-52 run at night and they dropped four 500-pounders on a bunker complex that another Recon team had found. Afterward, a spotter plane went over the site to check it out and it never returned. After some God-awful humping, we found the craters. I swear you could have built a two-story house in the crater and the roof would be just at ground level. It was like looking down into a volcano. We searched all day and found no plane and no bodies or parts thereof. We told G-2, at their urging, that we counted twenty-two confirmed NVA kills and no American. G-2, along with most "higher-ups," were told or encouraged to inflate enemy kills to enhance U.S. effectiveness. That is what I was told and now what I believe and understand. The grave registrar wasn't happy. He could have stayed at the site and looked more if he wanted to, it would have been fine with us.

Our excitement upon returning was founded on the word that Recon Battalion was getting a pallet of beer. Not only that, but we were to get real beef steaks and a cook-out. The beer arrived in the afternoon and was somehow divvied up between the four companies. They told us we'd each get two cans. So we lined up well before chow and got our ration of two beers. The beer was as warm, or warmer, than piss and when I opened the first one, it shot up and out of the can like a geyser. I had to gulp it. It went fast. I was going to save the other one for chow but the guys didn't so I followed their example. This time, we thumped the top and slowly popped the flip-top and the results were better; the 100° beer was great.

It was the first time two beers ever made me a little loopy and no one even asked me for an ID. I was still only 20 years old; my big birthday was still a couple of months away. When my friends arranged a nice pizza party at a local joint before I ended my leave, just before going to Viet Nam, they all bought a pitcher of beer. I couldn't buy one. I wasn't old enough. I was old enough to go to Nam, though.

Finally, we could smell the steaks cooking. There were long lines but the smell made it worth the wait. We each got a well-burned steak of some kind, pale greenish-yellow canned peas and the usual watery powdered mashed potatoes. We all pretended it was good. I had my first experience with a flying cockroach. We were all sitting around outside and, kerplop, right in my potatoes. I just stared at it in disbelief. It was huge, bigger than a grasshopper. It was struggling in my potatoes, either drowning or suffocating. Having already finished eating what they said was steak, I flung the potatoes, peas and cockroach in a gloppy mess to the ground. I wasn't taking any chances. That thing could have just flown in from the officers' latrine for all I know. I saw many more of the buggers after, but that was my first encounter with a flying cockroach. In Nam, all things that crawled and flew, venomous and poisonous, were big and nasty.

CHAPTER 11

The mission up on the Ben Hai River would not be much fun; we would be up tight against the river in no-man's land. The DMZ was a swath of land that was the separation between North and South Viet Nam and the Ben Hai River runs roughly through the middle of it and was used to delineate the DMZ. The "military" part of the demilitarized zone was a joke. Some shiny-starred generals drew the two lines on a map and said, "Neither the North Vietnamese Army nor American military shall enter or cross the DMZ." OK, Joe.

We went where we weren't supposed to go. But, all's fair in love and war, right?

There would be no choppers flying into the DMZ. It would be humping all the way in and back and I was hoping for a two-way mission. Again, where we went, the question wasn't if there were NVA, the question we had to answer was, were they on the move, amassing troops, what units, what types of weapons, and what kinds of supplies? G-2 wanted evidence and we had to get it.

That meant we had to bring back more than notes, we had to get real evidence, the kind of hard evidence that requires risk with no room for mistakes or guesses. We talked a lot and studied the map before we left the next morning. Sleep was intermittent and morning chow was ignored. Greased up in heavy warpaint, I guided the chopper in for a ride close to the DMZ.

One good thing in our favor was the terrain. There was no triple canopy in sight but it was thick with good canopy for cover. We considered triple canopy to be dense foliage consisting of smaller understory trees with taller canopy trees and the top layer of old growth giant trees. The sun penetrated the whole triple canopy with only subdued indirect light. It was stifling hot with little to no air movement and quiet, as only a jungle can be quiet. There were lots of birds. We didn't like birds, they sounded alarms or went silent, another clue that someone was approaching. It worked both ways, for the NVA and us, but we liked the quiet. The hills were not terribly steep but gave us valleys to traverse. We found a main trail right away but got nervous. So, we walked parallel to the trail, intersecting from time to time. We were headed straight toward the big river deep inside the DMZ. Jesus, Joseph and Mary.

We neither saw nor heard anything the first day but we could feel it. They were there. Could they sense our presence? We would be very unexpected guests. The NVA took nothing for granted either and we knew it. The trail was easy walking so we slowly – very slowly – continued on the well-worn trail to give us a little rest. We knew, sooner or later, there would be traffic.

Bart's tight fist was in the air. We froze. We all heard talking at the same time as Bart's hand sliced through the air down and away. Take cover, just like in the drills. On our bellies on both sides of the trail we lay, but not opposite each other. The talking was louder and then they were there. Three uniformed NVA with backpacks headed our way with rifles over their shoulders, their hands on the barrel. They had not a care in the world. It seemed apparent they were alone. Just like in practice the plan was executed. When the lead man passed Bart, there was a loud crack, followed by two more almost simultaneously. Three

NVA dropped to the ground in death - just like that. Bart had the lead man. It was his call whether to shoot or not. John had the second man in line and if there was a third, Nick had a bead on him. If there were four or more NVA, they got a free pass and we stayed low and quiet to let them pass. My job was to flip my M-16 on full automatic and be ready. If there was a miss, I could not. There were no misses. Juan, with his M-79, hit the trail at a quick pace in the direction they came from. At the first bend in the trail, he stepped off into cover to watch. The four of us sprang to the trail and went to work. Pointing my rifle at the NVA in the middle, I placed the heel of my boot on his torso and pushed him over. He was dead.

I dropped to my knees, laid my rifle on the ground and slipped my K-bar, long blade knife, from its sheath. My first slice was the patch on his uniformed shoulder. Then off came another below the first. Nothing in the shirt pockets except cigarettes. His pants pocket revealed a couple of coins, pocket knife, wet matches and a small wallet. All these went with the patches on a pile.

Inside his shirt was a small map with gook writing in pencil. Bingo! I rolled him again and slipped off his pack and put the pile of stuff into the pack. Nick and I swung him off the low side of the trail, about 20 feet away and covered him with leaf litter and debris. At the same time, the other two dead soldiers were also hidden.

We lifted their packs up, scuffed the trail a little and disappeared into the jungle. Juan did not return immediately, but joined us about ten minutes later. The entire action didn't take more than five minutes. Teamwork, clockwork, precision execution, we carried out the Third Recon mantra - swift, silent, deadly. That was what we trained for, that was what we did. At 20 years old, we were expert assassins, without hesitation, guilt or remorse. We weren't bloodthirsty, hideous maniacs. No, we were trained Recon Marines somewhere in Nam fighting a war and trying to stay alive. We fulfilled our mission according to the rules of engagement with a sense of duty and precision.

We slowly made our way roughly parallel with the trail for a short distance, and then sat to rest and listen. After some time of absolute silence, we sipped water and consolidated the three packs. The contents that would be useful to G-2 in our debriefing were put in our own packs. The remaining items, like personal photos, ammo and small containers of rice were put back in the NVA packs and covered with jungle floor litter.

We moved on with care. We marked the location on our maps where the ambush had occurred with a small "x" which would mark the exact location of three North Vietnamese soldiers. The map would eventually be thrown out and the families would never know where the "x" was. Five hundred yards away, there was a buried backpack with the family photos and other personal effects. At the time, no thought of any of that occurred to us. Our focus was, why were they there, where had they come from. Were they going far or just over the next hill to join 200 comrades in a battalion of NVA's in a bunker complex, preparing to meet up with another 1,500 NVA to form a division of NVA to attempt to overrun a Marine Corps base camp in Quang Tri? If they were there, we would find them; that's where our focus was. We would need stealth, absolute perfection in our movements and a healthy dose of luck to live two more days, complete our mission and rendezvous with a chopper at the LZ.

I should have taken a minute to radio Walter Cronkite, as we had to keep an accurate account of enemy killed. "Hi, Walter, this is Norm from 3-C-2 calling. Please add three enemy killed to the list for your body count show tonight. Yep, three confirmed kills. Oh, please call the President for us. Tell Lyndon he can send out three more 'Sorry about that but this is war' letters to the families of the three NVA we killed. Tell Lyndon not to give the coordinates of where they are, it will give our position away. Just say they are in the jungle in the DMZ. Yeah, that's right, from Nuts, right 2, down 1. And while I've got you on my radio, our infantry unit 1/9 took hill 238 today for the third time this month. They killed 30 NVA and nine Marines were killed. Names? Nah, don't know the names. It doesn't matter, just report the numbers." Too bad, we must have had a bad connection. Walter reported 300 NVA were killed, not 30. I told him nine Marines died but he thought I said none. Oh, well. Shit happens.

We made a loop towards the northwest end of our coverage zone and planned to loop around to be at the LZ the next day. It gave us plenty of time and that was good because we almost ran smack dab into the middle of the proverbial hornet's nest. We crouched and crawled far enough in to see that there were what seemed like gazillions of NVA uniforms in an organized rest stop. They were on the move and they looked tired. They were lugging lots of heavy weaponry and the heat must have sapped their energy. The three we killed were some sort of forward scouts or something. But they weren't doing their job.

We had seen enough, we backed off ever so slowly. We knew we could circle around, cross the trail hours before they got there and head southeast away from the river and to the LZ. Pussyfoot we did but dally we did not.

My, oh my, that chopper sounded wonderful as it made a tight circle and landed just outside the bank of yellow smoke. We were anxious to get out of there. We handed over our evidence and report to the G-2 boys. Mess hall, here we come. Bombs were dropped again that night, for sure.

CHAPTER 12

Another malaria pill down the hatch. At least we didn't get the shots anymore. My shot card was almost filled up before my arrival in Da Nang four months ago. I was needled and shot with vaccines twenty-nine times. At Camp Pendleton in California, we went through a line of corpsmen with high pressure guns that shot the stuff into our arms and shoulders. It was like some kind of hazing ritual. I admit that it hurt. By the time we were half way through, our arms were puffed up, red and bleeding. I guess there wasn't the concern about contamination and sterile application back in 1968. They used no alcohol wipes or anything sterile. We were like cattle, just move 'em through. The next two days were pretty painful and we could hardly raise our arms, but we lived through it. It's probably a good thing we had all that medicine pumped into us; there was a big potential to get some dreaded disease or infection in Nam.

The pouring rain just didn't stop. We were scheduled to go out one day but the choppers couldn't fly, so we got some extra time to sleep in. The driving rain on the galvanized tin roof was deafening yet hypnotic. I closed my eyes and remembered the thunderstorms when I was a kid in my beloved town of Ashfield, Massachusetts. Back then I didn't mind going down to the ravine in the rain to do a little fishing, the air smelled so good and the fish were more active. Or, I'd go up the steep stairs to the second floor in the room where a rare guest would stay overnight. It was right next to Gramp's bedroom and the pipe smoke smelled so good. I'd read comics on the bed, listening to the rain and thunder. There was a screen in the window all summer. It was just a short screen, but it sounded just like being outdoors. I'd fall asleep and be awakened by the birds singing, and sunshine coming through the window. I was a homesick twenty-year-old Marine lying on a canvas cot in Nam trying to escape my new world and the realization that I was trapped in a world I didn't like, a life of fear, killing, discomfort and death. How innocent life was for a twelve-year-old.

Nick would be leaving soon. He was a short-timer. With any luck, he'd have just one more mission and away he'd go on the big silver bird that would spirit him away from evil and into the world, home, the United States of America. He showed off his short-timer calendar every day as he penciled in another little box, a box symbolizing hope and freedom. Just nine more days to go for Nick. That's great. We were happy for him.

Being already scheduled to go out but being halted by the rain for three days, Nick was really apprehensive about this last mission. What if? But, fate intervened. The first sergeant was the best of the best, he took care of his men, although sometimes taking care of us meant yelling and spitting for an infraction we committed. But, he was nonetheless our nanny and protector while in his charge. Every team that walked up the little road of "C" Company and past the office and first sergeant quarters on our way to the unknown, he was always there to salute us and say, "God speed, men." He never missed. We looked forward to that. It meant a lot to us.

We heard that the rain would end that night and we'd go out the next morning. A runner came down to say the first sergeant wanted to see Nick. It must have been divine intervention for him. He came back very excited. With six days left, he would not go out with us. He was going home. With paperwork to do and going to Da Nang to get on a scheduled flight to anywhere, USA, he was relieved of duty with 3-C-2.

We sure would miss him. He was a good man to have by your side. Nick packed more stuff into an already full seabag. He wanted to party all night but we had to put a damper on it. The next morning we said our good-byes. We were all greased and geared up. We all shook hands with Nick and away we went. We all knew we'd never see him again. How odd military life could be. You got to know someone so well. You seemed to know his whole family, even the favorite meal his mother cooked.

We went into the jungle together like brothers. We had each other's backs. The closeness and camaraderie were heightened by the war. We made promises to always keep in touch, knowing full well that we never would. If we lived through all of this, we'd be stationed somewhere, who knew where, or we'd be discharged and go on with life. Nick wasn't sure if he would go back to Puerto Rico where he was born or settle in Florida and be a cop. I wonder what ever happened to Nick. I never heard from him. Many years later I tried to find him but never did. About thirty years after the USMC, I did locate John, Bart and Juan. I joined the Third Recon Battalion Association and they had contacts for many of us.

With Doc, we had our five guys and went somewhere out in the jungle. The missions seemed to blend into each other. It was the same jungle, the same ants, bugs and creatures and NVA all wanting to kill us. All that changed were the coordinates and the shape and size of the LZ. They were all small, dangerous, and when the chopper squeezed into the small opening of an LZ, it was like squeezing through the gate to hell.

The close call of that mission was caused by Doc. Bart halted movement and we dispersed off the trail. We all heard, or thought we heard, voices. There wasn't a bus station nearby so it was probably some bad guys not on our Christmas card list. We waited and waited. All of a sudden Doc started to sneeze. The first one caught him by surprise and was bad. He muffled the following two sneezes. We thought for sure there would be a firefight. It was a good thing we were spread out a little. If we had to shoot, it would have been going at them from different directions and they might think there were more Americans than there was. It was quiet and quieter. Holy shit! They never heard us! After about an hour we regrouped. If, and that's an if, they did hear us, they would probably split up. One group would circle around on the opposite side of the trail from the noise and set up an ambush. The other group would do the same up ahead. We studied the map and decided to travel perpendicular to the trail, turn towards a path parallel to where we were originally going and continue on our mission. We were pretty confident that in our travels during the next three days we would again see them or their friends.

We did not see anything extraordinary for the duration of our patrol although we saw plenty of evidence of human activity, like a bivouac location, fresh tracks in the mud, but no NVA. I was happy to see the chopper swooping down on us. Upon departing the chopper, we did our routine gesture to the pilot and his crew. We always gave a salute and thumbs up sign. It wasn't a formal, stand up straight salute, but a salute nonetheless. Being semi-crouched with soft cover (hat) and rifle in hand, the gesture was one of appreciation and job well done. We always got a thumbs up and a smile in return.

The chopper pilot, co-pilot and two gunners were, for the most part, great guys. They have come in to get us in hot LZ's when enemy fire left many, many holes in a good helicopter. They have risked crashing in LZ's that were almost too small or had broken trees that prevented them from a ground landing. They used finesse to lift us out and up while we dangled from a rope. And they always found us out in some God forsaken spot like the proverbial needle in a haystack. They came out once or twice in fog and rain when we didn't expect them to fly. They did their job very, very well. There was a lot of mutual respect. We never saw much of the accompanying gunship crew, but they too were right in the thick of it. When we had to dash into the open in a hot LZ with explosions and gunfire worse than imaginable, the gunship always seemed to be banking at the right place and time to lay down a gauntlet of fire with two 50-caliber machine guns and a couple of pod missiles to protect our asses.

There was one time in particular that we had what we considered a short distance mission. From Stud (Vandergrift) it was only about a ten-minute ride out to our insertion point. I believe we were looking for evidence of NVA build-up.

There was always fear of a base being overrun. And, with Stud being a main helicopter depot and central communications command, all the fuel tanks and aircraft were vulnerable. It was only a two-day stint to recon the zone. The terrain was a little too open for our liking and there had been previous battles around there before and large holes of open areas were hard to avoid. It was frightening to feel like a fish in an aquarium; you wondered who was looking in.

We couldn't see them but we could feel their presence. We got hit the first night. That is to say, where we were at dark, not where we had moved to; a perfect example of why a Recon team always moves after dark. It was a rather breezy, restless night, never quite quiet; we were uneasy and sleepless. Sometime after midnight we smelled pot. Quite often the gooks would smoke pot before an attack; I suppose it got them psyched up, but it was a tip-off. I never knew why they did that, why let themselves be detected by the smell of marijuana, they were so disciplined in every other way. We all nudged each other and quietly got on one knee, at the ready. All of a sudden it sounded like the world was coming to an end. About 300 feet away, right where we had been at dark, small arms, automatic AK-47 fire and two grenades tore up the whole area. It lasted about fifteen seconds and it was quiet. It was nerve-racking quiet.

We then heard the human chatter. It sounded like they were going away. Apparently, they didn't have a light, which we didn't have either. They must have decided their job was done and the dead Americans could lie there to rot. That was good for us. It seemed we would live for another day. We would not sleep tonight but we would live. The next day we found them.

We never saw a soul but we heard a great deal of bustle and milling around in the thick woods ahead. We were in decent cover but it opened up and then thick again where they were. They picked a great spot in an oasis with almost a 360° moat of open terrain around them. It would be suicide to attempt a closer look. Since none of us were prone to suicide, we backed off, found a nice little hill with good cover and sat out the day.

We figured we must be about two hours away from our pre-arranged extraction point the next afternoon. I called in to the relay station that we had fulfilled the mission and requested extraction before dark. I had already radioed in the events of the previous night. As predicted, we were denied extraction that day. No choppers were available. But extraction would be priority the next day at 0700 hours.

We chose a spot to move after dark and studied the terrain on the route. It was Godawful hot and the ants almost made us move; those little buggers sure could bite. Between the ants and the mosquitoes, we were restless and moved our arms too much. The entire night was quiet.

At first light we were anxious to move and get some real estate between us and the oasis boys. Juan dropped back a little farther than usual. We hesitated two or three times to compare maps and agree on our location. We figured we had one half hour to LZ with one hour before rendezvous.

Sometimes the choppers weren't exactly on time. If they were early, I'd wave them off from circling over the LZ site and if late we'd be ready with a smoke cannister and I'd zip them in. We decided to just get there and hide and wait. Juan came up behind us quickly and signaled with two fingers to his eyes. They were following us. He held up seven fingers and shrugged. Shit, there may be more. We moved. If we had to fight, do it where we chose and have some hope of escape.

Soon after, we took fire. It was a spray of small arms fire intended to rattle us and get us on the move. They wanted us out in the open and making mistakes. We got to the vicinity of the LZ without doing either. We had cover but no height advantage. I called in "contact" and asked for ETA of extraction. They were on the way. We wanted to believe them.

We stopped and they stopped. We waited and they waited. Good, maybe a little truce until our bus arrived. But, no way man. We started taking fire. Did they have enough men to get behind us, too? It didn't matter, we had nowhere to go. I sympathized with General Custer. I could hear the old boy say, "Sucks, don't it?"

We returned fire and I radioed "contact" again. "Taking fire at LZ." I reached up behind my shoulder and moved the knob clockwise seven clicks. "Aircraft, this is Ringlet, do you copy, over?"

"Ringlet, this is Atlas. I have you. What is your position, over?"

"Ringlet at LZ taking fire, over."

"Roger, Ringlet. We're on the way. We're a short way out."

We continued to exchange fire, but it wasn't up close and personal. It was more like they weren't hungry for the kill until they knew how many they had and the time was right. I was sure their delay was to get in better position. But their plan was foiled. I heard the rotor blades – whump-whump-whump – in the distance.

"Atlas, this is Ringlet. Head west and confirm LZ, over."

And there he was, a beautiful green helicopter coming in over the trees. I gave him the "Mark, Mark" call to let him know he was directly overhead.

"I have you, Ringlet. My next pass will be for pick-up."

"Roger, Atlas."

He made a wide, high circle and came down and in, straight at us. The gunship continued on and began a run above and perpendicular to our ride.

"Smoke going out, Atlas," I radioed and threw out a green smoke cannister as far as I could. A smoke cannister is about the same size and weight as a 16 ounce can of beer, maybe a little lighter. John saw right away that the breeze was from our way to the enemy position, so he threw another smoke to give us a little screening.

"Atlas, enemy on your port, Recon on starboard."

Just then, the port side gunner started in with the rapid fire 50-caliber gun. The pilot, the co-pilot and two gunners all had headsets on to communicate, so all could hear me. Just before touchdown, we made our move and ran for the chopper. At the same time, the gunship came swooping across with machine guns blazing and two rockets on their way to the sweet spot enemy location.

We were taking hits like crazy and it seemed forever for enough lift to get going. The sound of bullets hitting the chopper was loud and terrifying.

In good air, we left the scene but we weren't doing very well, it was not smooth. The quick drops and rotor movement was erratic; something was very wrong. We were lumbering and had trouble keeping altitude but it could be that the pilot wanted to get lower.

It was a good thing the ride was a short distance from Stud because smoke started spewing from the engine just about the time we were approaching the wire perimeter of the airbase.

We barely made it over the wire and we were going too fast and too low, and instead of the usual slow descent down to the ground, we ended up plowing down and forward. What a ride! It was like an airplane with pontoons landing on a lake. When we came to a stop, the crew bailed out almost as fast as we did. We all just stood back and stared as the green whirlybird whined down to stillness. And then we all laughed and give high fives to each other. We congratulated and thanked the crew for saving our butts. We all examined the ship. The pilot put a hand on the rear stabilizer rotor and shook it. "It isn't supposed to do that," he said.

We counted twenty-three holes in the fuselage. We all walked away together as two jeeps were tearing at us. The pilot told us that a crane helicopter would pick up the mortally wounded chopper and take it over to the maintenance hangar to be cannibalized for parts. A crane helicopter looks a little like a praying mantis. The whole middle is open and had a chain and hook with a hydraulic lift to carry large objects like light jeeps and huge piles of ammo and supplies in netting.

It was a close call all around. We were suddenly hungry and very tired. We were coming down from a pretty intense time of it. Damn, we were lucky.

Back at C Company, there seemed to be a lot of hubbub with lots of guys milling around. Then we heard the horrible news. Little did we know that while we were duking it out for our lives, 3-C-1 got wiped out. Jesus, Joseph and Mary. No, say it ain't so.

About two out of ten missions resulted in some sort of confrontation with the enemy, and with some teams it was even more, depending on the nature of the mission. 3-C-1 had contact just before dark and made a stand on the knoll where they were. There would be no extraction because they could not break free to get to an LZ. Claymore mines were hastily set up right at their position and they waited. They were overrun in the middle of the night.

Guys were saying they could hear much of what was going on at our comm-shack. It was horrible and nothing could be done. There was yelling and pleas for help, explosions and gunfire. The radio operator, Fred, said they were done. Everyone was hit and the NVA left them all for dead. Fred and Danny and a new team leader named Andy Wise lived and later told the whole story. They were actually in hand-to-hand combat. That means K-bar knives and rifle butts and bare knuckles. In the end, you just collapsed under overwhelming numbers and played dead or were dead.

Fred Ostrum's life was saved by Robert Jenkins. An NVA grenade was thrown near Ostrum and Jenkins immediately threw himself over Ostrum as the grenade exploded. Jenkins was killed instantly. Fred was very seriously hurt but lived. Robert was the Marine's Marine and he looked like Big John, a giant of a man that Recon guys knew well. He sacrificed his life for his teammates. He would later be awarded the Congressional Medal of Honor posthumously. He was from Florida and there is a street, a school and a post office named in his honor. The Third Recon Battalion Association gives a scholarship every year in his honor. A part of our dues and donations keeps that scholarship alive.

Danny also lived and remarkably had only minor wounds. He returned to 3-C-1 as part of a new, rebuilt team. Danny was everybody's best friend, he was always upbeat and singing his favorite song, "Sittin' on the Dock of the Bay," over and over. We'd have to tell him to stop it. He was from the Bronx and said many times, "When I get out of here, I'm going down to the docks to work and sing all day."

Danny would leave but it would be in a military metal casket. He lived through that terrible ordeal of hand-to-hand combat but two months later he would die from a single gunshot wound to the stomach, standing behind me while defending our team. He never saw the docks again. I miss him even after fifty years. As a matter of fact, it is exactly fifty years (2018) since my time in Viet Nam.

There was a solemn ceremony for Robert Jenkins; his rifle with mounted bayonet was stuck in the ground with his boots neatly standing behind his rifle. The padre said a few words, as well as our

Company Commander, Captain Randall. Our first sergeant dismissed us and we went back to our hooches to prepare for the next mission. We all went to the First Aid Station to visit Danny.

Miraculously, Danny had only six or seven shrapnel wounds and would return to us in a few days. The nut was actually ready and willing to come back right away to rebuild "his" team. He was somber about Jenkins and saw him jump on Fred before the grenade exploded. Danny was thrown down by the explosion and was knocked out.

The next day the milling around continued. Those of us who went over to visit Danny and Wise got bits and pieces of what happened and, with the radio transmissions that some heard, we all tried to fill in the blanks. It didn't really matter, I suppose. Except, we always talked about what we did right to replicate and what we didn't do so well to improve after every mission. 3-C-1 didn't seem to do much wrong, it was just wrong place and wrong time to be seen. Recon teams are always vulnerable, teams aren't invisible and they had to move, they had to get close. Training and experience were the best in the world but all of that can't always stop bad things from happening. In war, shit happens.

During our discussions, the subject of war came up and I was all ears. I hadn't really thought about our role in my five months there. I concentrated on team, focus, mission and staying alive. We were a unit, we were tight, we were damned good. We were an isolated community, our daily routine was preparing for the next mission and our next mission was a life in itself. We didn't ask why, only where and when. We were Marines, not politicians. We were at war, right? Or, were we? Some of the guys started talking about letters from home and friends. There were protests against the war at colleges.

Politicians were asking for peace talks. Viet Nam was a quagmire. General Westmoreland was lying to the public and Walter Cronkite's body count was bullshit. What?

It all seemed a little overwhelming to me. Why didn't we know all this before? Once I heard all that, it got some of us to thinking about our role. Okay, so we did our job. We went out and found enemy strongholds. We came back with locations, sometimes prisoners, maps, documents and unit patches. But it was over and over again. We'd come back and report our mission to the bright boys and they'd send grunts out to kick ass or send the B-52s out to make holes in the ground. And then they would leave. The NVA would come back, we'd go out and find them and the grunts would go back out and kick ass. Our body count went up on every hill we fought to take for the third time. Now that you put it that way, what the fuck! What was it all about?

WWII was a war to win. Americans landed with the Marines in front. They went through Sicily, Italy, France to Germany and when Hitler was dead, Americans planted a flag on his headquarters and said, we won. When those Jap sons-of-bitches bombed Pearl Harbor, we did the same thing until their big orange meatball flag was thrown overboard and they signed an unconditional surrender. It was a long, bloody war and we lost thousands of American lives. But in the end, it was the Stars and Stripes attached to a pole and the guns stopped shooting and men stopped dying. There were huge parades and celebrations. The soldiers were welcomed home to glorious victory. The world was at peace. The holocaust was over, the Japs were defeated and democracy and freedom prevailed.

"Geez," someone piped in, "why don't we get all the Marines and the Army, line up and walk north with every fuckin' gun, artillery, plane and weapon we have. Kill every fuckin' one of those little slant-eyed, rice-propelled bastards that doesn't run away. When we get to Hanoi, we hunt down that ol' bastard with the white beard they call Uncle Ho and slit his throat and call it a day." "Yeah," said another, "we'll raise the flag over his house and say, we're going home. We won."

We wished life were that simple. We seemed more confused the more we talked. We decided that maybe our generals and President knew what they were doing. We're Recon. We just had to live up to our end of the bargain and do what we're told. In the end, all would be well. We heard the peace talks were going on. Ho Chi Minh had probably had enough. We would probably be out of there before long. We hoped Danny would be back soon. We tried to help 3-C-1 get their act together as a new team. The first sergeant saved a spot for Danny in the team. They sure needed him, more than ever.

CHAPTER 13

I discovered that my meritorious promotion to lance corporal added about 73¢ to my monthly paycheck of $78. At that rate, I was thinking of retiring in luxury or maybe opening my own business. Funeral directors always had plenty of work. Regardless of the promotion, no one wore rank insignias at base camp and certainly not out on patrol.

More rain. I was so in awe of the rain. I had never before seen such rain in New England, not even close. It was relentless. During such torrents, it was not uncommon to just skip the mess hall. Standing, walking and sitting in the jungle in such rain was unavoidable, but standing in line at the mess hall was not. If I was lucky, there'd be a can of boned chicken left, and there was usually a case or two of C-rations in a corner somewhere.

We had paperback books the guys would get in the mail and we would pass them all around to share. It was a reasonable distraction, that and writing a letter home about nothing would take a whole afternoon. And, of course, sleep was good, too. Rain crashing on the tin roof was loud but also hypnotic.

Out to the chopper pad for another mission. And then another one after that. On the last time out, it was the second day and we took a break next to a small clearing. It was my turn to rest and I sat down and compared my location on the map with John's. Good, we agreed.

I leaned against my pack, sipped some water and unbuttoned my shirt, but it didn't help a great deal. The air was thick and heavy and the heat bore down into me. I pulled my wet shirt apart and closed my eyes. I rarely fell asleep during my rest breaks but I did that day.

The guys saw what happened, held their breath, and were thankful I didn't wake up. When I was nudged awake, they told me that while I slept, the largest centipede they'd ever seen crawled up my side, crawled over the folds of my shirt, across my bare chest and down the other side.

"Norm, if you had felt it and instinctively tried to brush it away, that big ol' centipede would have bitten you and you would have been one sick dude," Bart said. "That thing could have killed you. It was like a 100-legged snake, no shit." What Bart had done was wait until the huge creature crawled away from me, then cut its head off with the K-bar and tossed it into the jungle because he didn't even want me to see how big it was. Thank the Lord for small favors.

Doc had been going out with 3-C-1, but only recently because replacements were in short supply. Between guys rotating out, guys getting jungle-type sicknesses and 3-C-1 being decimated, they didn't have the manpower next door to go out. As a result, we did more duty with only one to two days rest in between missions. But "C" Company got three replacements all at once. They moved Doc next door to 3-C-1, we got a new guy and the others went somewhere.

Now I knew how they felt getting a new guy to replace someone they trusted and loved. His name was Phil Sawyer and he was from Alaska, a pretty rugged guy, short and stocky, and he looked strong. He also looked very young. Did he finish high school, I wondered?

We didn't have much time to get him prepped and ready and I felt badly because a lot of stuff was jammed at him in two days. But he seemed to take it in stride and seemed anxious to be part of the team.

Out at the ammo dump, we outfitted him with his armaments, walked past the ol' Sarge's shack with a fresh snake nailed to the wall which Phil never even noticed, and we walked to the pad to wait for our ride.

I had a feeling we weren't going out. It was foggy with a heavy mist; they couldn't fly today, I figured. I was wrong. In came our ride, a big ol' CH-46 with the hydraulic tailgate, extra crew, and a crew chief to guide the pilot in. The big chopper had two rotors on top and was slow and clumsy. It was also louder and took too much time to get up and out of the LZ. But it worked, I guess.

We couldn't see the ground on our approach to the LZ until we were a couple of hundred feet from landing. We always liked to have a visual so we could see the terrain and know where to head first after we dropped from the chopper.

After we dropped, I waved the pilot away and we moved quickly to get away from the LZ. The weather was the same there, if not worse, the fog thicker. It was eerie quiet. Our cover was okay but not great. It was like a second-growth forest and the terrain was flat, too flat. It was hard to determine just where we were so we had to look at our maps more often. Bad start. It didn't look right, nothing seemed to fit and after only four or five hours, we had the feeling that we had no clue where we were. Great! Maybe we'll get a glimpse of a high rise through a break in the fog or we might run into some gooks and they'll probably know where we are and point us in the right direction. Or, we could have just wandered around for a month or two until the grave registrars came a lookin'. It was not fun.

G-2 had identified what they thought would be a large, well-worn trail for us to check out. We expected to intercept it, but no dice. That's it, at the next phone booth, I was going to call AAA.

Lost in the jungle was a great way to get in trouble fast. Add to that thick fog, rain and flat terrain and we were concerned.

A little while later we found the trail and followed it to the first sharp turn. Looking at the map, we discovered we weren't that far off but we'd best check frequently. The scene reminded me of an old movie about an expedition out in the Amazon hiding from the headhunters.

We got nervous walking on a well-worn trail in the jungle, so we peeled off to do a big loop and reconnect later. It worked fine but the rain got worse. We saw a large knoll ahead so we parked ourselves some distance from it and moved there after dark.

The following morning and throughout the next day it was more of the same weather. We checked our location on the map frequently but felt as though we were always on the ragged edge of being lost most of the time.

It was very late afternoon, more like early evening, Juan came up tight and stopped us. Two fingers at his eyes meant he had a visual of the enemy. He held up one finger. So, there was one NVA, but when there's one there's usually lots more.

We dispersed and, after an hour, saw and heard nothing. We could see a large knoll to the east, well off the trail and decided we had to make it there.

When we stood up, we all saw two gooks on the trail creeping our way. They ducked off the trail after seeing us at the same time that we saw them.

"Let's go for it," John said, and we took off at a slow run. The knoll was further away than it looked. I was wicked winded and by the time we got to the top of the nub; we were all practically hyperventilating.

It was fairly decent cover with some rocks for extra defense. We took our packs off and put them in the middle of us. I put two grenades in front of me on a rock and I had 450 bullets in twenty-five magazines hooked to my harness. I whispered in our situation and gave our position from the "Nuts" reference point.

There was little doubt that we were compromised. It would be a long night. All I could think about was 3-C-1.

From my rock, I kept a steady eye out ahead. I saw movement, then a gook dash across the trail into cover. I held fire as John had instructed before, and besides, it happened too fast anyway. Another one did the same thing but hesitated on the trail to look our way and I had him and almost pulled the trigger when he dove away.

Right after dark, Bart and John each pulled out a claymore mine from their packs. Bart crawled out and down in front of me to set a mine out facing the trail. John gave the other one to Phil and told him to do the same on the opposite side but Phil wouldn't take it, he just stared at John. So John crawled out himself, set the mine and, like Bart did, unwound the line to our position and put the end squeeze trigger on a pack.

Phil was lying next to the packs in a fetal position and gently weeping. Great. We're fresh out of bottles of warm milk to give him. There was no sympathy, there wasn't the time or energy to baby him. John whispered to him to get up. We needed him. It would be fine.

It was a no go, Phil was done and wouldn't move.

All night we waited and listened and strained our eyes. All night was rain and rolling fog and quiet. We couldn't believe it. They just disappeared. Every hour we got sit reps but there was no sleep or radio watch.

At first light, Phil was curled up and sleeping. Bart and John crawled out to retrieve the claymores. We put our heads together and John laid out our situation moving ahead. If we left now, we couldn't make it to the LZ in time for our ride. It had to be rescheduled. No luck there, no choppers would fly that day. The gooks had seen us and probably knew just about how many of us there were. They appeared to have left. So why didn't they hit us last night? Were they too short on numbers? Were they on their way somewhere and just didn't want to take the time to mess with us? Did they move further down the trail on both ends and set up an ambush for us? No way would we go on a trail. We had to hope the weather would clear later. Phil huddled with us but couldn't look us in the eyes. He was ashamed. Some people just don't have it and he knew it.

Our plan was to make a wide circle around, away from the trail, and miraculously come out at the LZ, which was a different one than our insertion point. It stopped raining but the fog and mist prevailed most of the day. I inquired three times about extraction. No birds would fly.

Early that afternoon was quiet, the fog was lifting and it was a little brighter. We had no visuals of human activity either. When we came out to where the LZ should be, we were again disappointed. We agreed to split up. Two guys went southwest and two guys northeast and we agreed to meet back at the spot of departure in one hour or less. Phil was instructed to sit tight, don't move and be quiet. He agreed. John and I went in opposite ways so each group would have a map. Juan and I got back in just over an hour. John and Bart found our LZ. Once we got close enough to see well, we noticed a dead tree practically in the middle of it. No chopper could land there. Relay Tango advised of extraction on-going. Wow. A chopper was coming.

An hour later we heard the symphony we wanted to hear but we could tell just by the sound it was a CH-46, the large lumbering chopper. A smaller helicopter just might have squeezed in the space but not that big boy.

Bart hurriedly removed his pack and got out a plastic bag with detonation cord and fuse. Once I had a visual and made contact, I advised the pilot to circle once while we blew a tree.

Bart ran out, wrapped the cord, set the fuse and ran back. It blew and fell. Juan threw a smoke and I called the pilot in. It seemed to take forever for the tailgate to come down but it did and up we went. To our surprise, we began to take fire. It was not a big deal. The gunner on that side opened up and three of us began shooting out the window for a few seconds before we were out of there. So those buggers were still in the area and watching the LZ.

John stopped off at the "C" Company office while we hit the showers. Later, after evening chow, a runner came by to tell Phil to get his gear. There was a jeep leaving to take him to I-9. That was an infantry unit closest to Quang Tri. Phil would not stay with Recon. We said our goodbyes and wished him well. You're either Recon or not. There are no second chances.

CHAPTER 14

Bart was getting short, his calendar pretty well colored in. I couldn't imagine not having Bart at point. Good news, though. Danny would be coming back the next day. We missed him and I haven't heard his terrible rendition of "Sittin' on the Dock of the Bay" in ages, it seemed. Strangely enough, I missed it.

Up until the Korean War, men went to war and stayed the duration. Now, men are shuttled in and out to perpetuate the longevity of the whole mess.

Another trip to a relay station for us. Why us? We were to go to India Relay, a small pinnacle top mountain with a cave-like bunker for radio watch and sleeping quarters for a lieutenant who was in charge. The rest of us would sleep one step down in a dug-out hole lined with ammo boxes and a roof of slats with more ammo boxes and an oiled canvas tarp over the top. It was small with about four feet of head room. Two people slept in each dug-out on top of an ammo box bed. There were three of the little crude dug-outs.

When we got there, I had to run new wire to the antenna, which I had to reset and move. The courier wire deteriorated quickly in that environment and from being stepped on. I fixed that, too, and moved the wire over the top of the command bunker under sandbags.

There were three mortar pits. We brought about 30 mortars with us. We all had to practice sliding the mortar down the tube and then readjusting the angle to walk it in front of the gooks attempting to overrun the position. There was quite a tangle of concertina wire around us and below that was a steep bank all around that was mined. When we finished a C-ration meal, we just threw the cans over the bank. What a mess it was, like a dump. And, of course, the New York City rats clamored all through the cans at night, sounding like an invasion of NVA. We also had illumination rounds for the mortar tubes. Every once in a while, at night someone would be positive we were being invaded and get permission to send up illumination. In two weeks, all we ever saw were rats.

It rained about all the time. We all took turns in the bunker on radio watch but, except for the guy out in the dark rain on watch, we usually all hung out in the bunker to read or play cards by the kerosene lantern. The nights in the cramped hole in the ground were especially awful, trying to sleep. The rats would come in at ground level and literally jump onto us and then onto what little dirt floor there was. It was unnerving having those rats on top of us and milling about. I think I would rather have been in the jungle.

With all the rain, we had to eat under cover and pretend to be a little dry once in a while. Outside in the rain, we were sort of dry because we had large heavy plastic ponchos, nice but hot. They made too much noise and took up too much room to take in our packs on a mission.

Night guard duty was so boring and wet; the rats rattled everything around on the side hills and it always sounded like humans. No respectable NVA soldier would ever get near the place. We played lots of card games for two weeks and our biggest worry was getting bitten by a rat. Without a chopper able to get in for days on end, a rat bite could have been a death sentence.

When we got back to 3-C-2, it seemed like a vacation, but a short one.

We had a young second lieutenant around and he was going out with teams. Everyone liked him, he was outgoing and got along with everyone. But, this trip, we had a Green Beret going out with us. He was a typical serious, better-than-thou Army dude. It was another long-range jobbie right on the Ho Chi Minh Trail.

The difference on that mission was that we crossed the Trail to higher ground so we could walk along a ridge until we could observe the compound of the NVA. It was a big one and trucks came in all night to unload; it was like a train station.

They did a great job of camouflage and unless looking specifically for something there, you'd probably never see it from the air. We knew it was big because we could hear it from afar. We kept getting closer until we had a good view, but it was a bit scary. Here we were in Laos, looking down into South Viet Nam. I wonder what ol' Walter Cronkite would report about that? LBJ would deny for an hour that we were there. Stop by any time, Lyndon, I'll save a pound cake for you and get you familiar with the map.

We verified and double-verified the exact coordinates of the compound. The B-52s would have a field day with that one.

Recon exchanged people from time to time with the Green Berets. They were all right but they were used to going out with larger groups. This guy had some C-4 and wanted to heat up some C-rations. He was nuts, man. He was fidgety and wanted to move out, he didn't have the patience to observe the routine of the place. There were guards out all the time but no night patrols, they were just passing through except for the officer in charge of the place and a few guards and women.

There was a lot of gear, food and ammo headed south. We were told there was a massive build-up again in the Central Highlands and further south down to the Delta. I hoped the bombs that fell after we got outta there would slow them down a touch.

Mr. Green Beret got his wish on the third day when we picked our time and went back down the ridge and across the Trail to our LZ rendezvous. It was clockwork perfect.

We didn't invite our friend to 3-C-2; we were sure it was too uncouth for him. He stayed on the chopper and went back to Stud to catch a ride back to his unit. We hoped he would get back before popcorn and the movies.

G-2 was thrilled to get the info and passed it up the chain of command. We bet that on that very night we would be glad we weren't anywhere near that NVA compound. Our little hooch suited us just fine.

CHAPTER 15

Two days later we had a two-day jaunt as a walk-in from Gio Linh. Walk-ins generally meant that we had more ground to cover. It also meant a different type of tactic to contend with. Viet Cong were beginning to terrorize the village. They snuck in at night to steal rice and convince the villagers to abandon any association with Americans. The VC gave villagers weapons to hide, taught those willing to help to set mines in roads and to steal from American GIs.

The VC were more mobile in that section of the jungle; they hid in tunnels with concealed trap door entrances and were a hit and run force to deal with. Small groups attempted ambush tactics to kill and maim, then disappear. We were hunted as much as we were hunting for them. They had lookouts and village sympathizers who would steal away from the village to tip the VC of our presence.

It seemed to make no sense to me to go in after them. For what purpose and what tangible result were we after? A five-man Recon team in a game of fight to the death? It was like going out to capture a handful of fog.

It was on that mission that I had a dreaded feeling which would haunt me all of my life. It was a nerve-tingling, sweaty palms, heart beating fast feeling of overwhelming fear that I was being watched. Somewhere out there, hidden and silent, were eyes upon me, studying every movement, calculating every step with the rifle sights lined up steady on my back.

It was difficult to shake, the consuming thoughts of an imminent loud crack of the rifle and the sudden drop of a body. It was as vivid as that last ambush where I did it to someone. I squeezed the trigger and heard the crack and watched the drop. I felt no fear then, no grip in the bottom of my stomach. I felt sweat and exaggerated heartbeat but I was the assassin, there was no remorse, no human compassion, only a target to put down swiftly and efficiently.

That is why I could not shake that powerful urge to hide and shield myself from the force about to put me down. Throughout my life I have, from time to time, been haunted by that feeling of eyes upon me. Sometimes it happened while deer hunting or in the woods on my path with my dog. I would have to quickly find a large tree behind which to hide myself and scan the woods. Slowly scan as I was taught -- never focus, always scan for movement and turn slowly to miss nothing. It didn't happen frequently but when it did I was transported back in time to those woods outside of Gio Linh. The feeling would always fade, I would come to an awareness of my surroundings as the trance faded away. And then I would look down to see my beautiful Border Collie, Sassy, sitting patiently and looking at me. If she could have talked, my little Sassy would say, "Come on, Dad, let's go." And we would.

We would go through life the best we could but never really entirely leaving the jungle. Never.

That mission, the one where the feeling of dread washed over me, turned out to be a walk in the woods. Maybe we were being watched for three days or maybe there was no one there to watch us. In my mind, they were there, they just didn't squeeze the trigger. I was exhausted both physically and mentally, and we had to wait two or three hours on the outskirts of the village because someone screwed up and a truck wasn't dispatched. As we waited, watching the villagers work the fields was soothing. They were bent over and ankle deep in muddy water pushing little rice sprouts into the mud. Long rows of the flooded fields were planted. Beyond them, more villagers walked behind water buffalo, making long straight rows. Dikes were reinforced and time stood still. All those poor villagers wanted was to be left alone; they were content with their simple lives. They had no morning newspaper or Saturday night at the movies, they didn't want guns or mines in their paths, they didn't love or hate Americans. And, they didn't know what communism was and probably never heard of Ho Chi Minh. It was quiet there, almost serene. I wish I'd had a cigarette.

CHAPTER 16

Back at base camp in Quang Tri, we just got to our hooch when Danny came out the door of our neighbor 3-C-1. The spring on the door snapped it shut with a slam.

"Hey, guys," Danny offered, "What's the good word?"

"No good word, Danny," John quipped, "only a shower, some chow and some sleep. What's up?"

And then he started; Danny was always upbeat and raring to go, even if there was nowhere to go. Danny then started a conversation that would forever change my life.

"We're going out tomorrow," Danny said. "It's an area that's seen a lotta shit. They think the gooks are moving back in because that whole area is like a big funnel for them to move down to the Central Highlands. We need you to come with us, Norm. We need you on the radio."

He was talking faster, like he didn't want me to interrupt him. "Don broke a finger," Danny continued. "He can't go with us and we need you to go."

Now he had my attention.

"Danny, he broke a finger?"

"Yeah," he replied. "We were running to the chopper and he tripped and fell."

"So, tell the pussy to suck it up," I quickly added.

"He can't, Norm. They said he can't go."

"Danny, read my lips, fuck you, I ain't going. You know how to use a radio, it ain't hard."

Danny didn't give up and had all the answers.

"We need the extra guy, Norm, we need you."

While we were bantering back and forth, John disappeared. I started treating the whole idea as a joke and continued to play the word game with Danny. My defense team even joined the fun, Juan suggestimg that maybe John Wayne or Audie Murphy might be free to go. The laughter and ribbing went on for a while as we unpacked and got ready to hit the showers.

John returned and put a damper on the whole party.

"Norm, after showers, go get your C-rations and check out a radio. You're going out with 3-C-1," John said in a soft but firm voice.

John had left to go see the first sergeant and he confirmed that the man had authorized me to go. We were short of men and the mission had to happen. I was pissed but there wasn't much I could do.

Gee, my plans were dashed. I had thought maybe after a relaxing soak in the tub and a full body massage, I'd get dressed up and go to the city with the guys. We could have hit a few nightclubs, had a big steak dinner and maybe catch a good movie before a nightcap. The chauffer surely wouldn't have minded a late night.

Danny knew all along that the First Sergeant had given the green light for me to go; I guess he just wanted me to come to it on my own. So, Danny and I did a little high-five and I told him I'd stop by after a shower. On my way, the thought occurred to me that Corporal Wise hadn't joined Danny to talk to me. He was the new team leader from Alpha Company who was a part of the team who endured that terrible battle. Wise was a quiet loner and we didn't know much about him except that he had been in Recon about six months, about the same as me.

So, after showers and picking up my radio, extra battery, and a case of C-rations, we went to evening chow. I stopped at 3-C-1 and reviewed the mapping with the guys. We went outside to compare compasses and I took my map and went next door to pack. The guys were playing cards when I lay my head down where I wished there was a pillow and went into a deep sleep. After what seemed like twenty minutes, my butler gently knocked on my door to awaken me. Actually, it was the bustle of guys getting up and the door slamming shut. I stared up as I lay there and realized I hadn't written home in a while. I wondered if I ever would again.

After the "good luck, Norm's," I went up our little street with 3-C-1 to early chow. Danny was singing "Sittin' on the Dock of the Bay" again. Someone suggested we all chip in for singing lessons for that poor boy. I smiled. It would be the last time Danny ever sang. Throughout the years and to this day, every time I hear that song played on the radio, I have either had a little smile or my eyes have welled up with the memory of that big goof-ball from the Bronx.

CHAPTER 17

Why was it that choppers were always early to pick us up for insertion and generally late to extract us? I made contact with the pilot and we were airborne.

The LZ was huge. It looked like it had been some sort of command center for choppers to bring in ammo and water and take out wounded. There were shell casings, half-rotted battle dressings and litter here and there.

Our mission assignment was a long and narrow stretch of desolate wasteland over large hills and along ridgelines to what looked like a very small opening on a bony ridge in very steep terrain. That opening would be our LZ for extraction in three days. That sucked! If we had wanted to, we could probably have been at that little opening in a day. To stay hidden in that terrain was a chore. Our progress was slow; we lingered in the heat surrounded off and on by good cover and used the binoculars to scan all around us. It was open woods and pecker brush for us but it was the same for any NVA foolish enough to want to be there.

The first day was encouraging, there was no sign of human activity and everything was quiet. Corporal Wise walked point which I didn't like but he seemed good at it. There were five of us after all. Wise walked point, followed by Second Lieutenant Shinault, who was the lieutenant we all liked, a pretty good dude who didn't pretend to be a general. He had been recruited by the first sergeant and happily obliged. Behind the lieutenant was the tall, lanky guy from Tennessee, McAffe. I even kidded him about being a big target. I followed behind him. Danny was the rear security guy but rather than carrying an M-79 like our Juan, he felt more at home with his M-16.

Our first night was quiet. I didn't like not moving after dark like we should and always did when John was in charge. I whispered to Wise my feelings just before dark. He just looked at me and whispered that we were fine. That was the end of that discussion.

Since we were less than twenty-five miles out from Stud, which was the Central Communications Command for Third Recon, there was no relay station interface. And, if within radio range of Stud, we would also have been in range of our Comm Shack at Quang Tri.

The next day our progress was slow but steady, the terrain was wicked steep and there were rocks and shale-like rock slides on the hillsides. I didn't like it. We maneuvered our way down one steep slope sliding on the loose rubble. There was a huge fallen tree that had been on the side hill for a long time and it was rotted. Going down over the rubble, I steadied myself with my left hand on the log. My arm began to burn and hurt. I looked down to see my arm covered with small ants chewing and biting me to bits.

With a rifle in my right hand, it was slow and awkward to brush them off; I even had to take my handball glove off to get them all. Danny thought it was funny.

"Fuck you," I whispered, as I stepped away from the dead tree with my red and swollen arm and half-slid the rest of the way down the hill. I wished the hell I had studied a little harder at Greenfield Community College. I'd be a famous engineer now with a big cigar and a cold gin and tonic, reviewing a complicated drawing and ordering all my subordinates to step it up a little. "Study hard," my parents used to say to me, "and good things will happen." They forgot to tell me about the dummies like me who didn't study hard and the bad things that would happen.

At the top of the next ridge, we blundered onto a good trail. It wasn't very wide and rutted like it had been used to transport wheel-mounted weapons, but it looked pretty well trod. The trick was, how to keep an eye on the trail without walking on it? The ridgelines were narrow and steep on both sides, and there was fifteen feet of brushy vegetation but no real jungle-type stuff to conceal five guys. The top of the ridge was only about fifty feet wide and some places a lot less than that.

Staying on the trail wasn't a good option and moving downhill from and parallel with the trail wasn't good either because it was noisy, too open and anyone on the trail would have a superior firepower advantage. So, we walked the trail. It was about mid-afternoon when we stopped to rest. The ridgeline flattened out some and we got off the trail and into decent cover.

After reviewing our maps, we agreed we could have reached our LZ by nightfall. But our rendezvous wasn't until afternoon of the next day. The question was, should we go check it out to see if it's suitable and hope we could find a safe place to spend the night and most of the next day or should we just hang out where we were?

We stayed in place nearby in a thick area downhill from the trail. I didn't like it and I could tell that Danny didn't like it either. The lieutenant was on the steep slope upward on the learning curve and Wise made the decision.

When officers went out with a Recon team, they were not in

charge, they acted as a rifle man in the middle of the team. The team leader always made the final decision on everything. In 3-C-2 we used consensus decision-making; it always seemed like we were in sync with each other. John was clearly the leader, but it seemed we all agreed that he had a knack for always having a solid plan and good ideas. Not often did we disagree or hesitate. We were tight. I realized that more than ever with 3-C-1, in that spot. There was no moving after dark again.

CHAPTER 18

It was a restless night of gentle but steady rain which stopped just before dawn. I removed the last can of food from my pack, a small tin of pound cake. With a little water, it was good. I pushed my heel into the dirt, making a small hole to scuff in the empty tin. As I bent over from a sitting position, the quiet morning air erupted into a thunderous roar of automatic gun fire. The leaves on the trees were shredding and debris was flying. I spun myself around, flipped my rifle selector on automatic and, while steadying my rifle on my pack, I let loose a full magazine of eighteen rounds.

Danny was the only one who stood up to shoot. The whole exchange took less than ten seconds and then it was quiet. It was a hit and run. No one was hit.

I radioed in the contact and called for extraction at the designated LZ. We did not confer or plan, we hurried up to the trail. There were no dead bodies or blood trails.

I received a transmission that advised us to find high ground and form a defensive position. That good advice was ignored. We stepped into our positions and, without knowing Wise's intentions, we started to move on the trail in the direction of the LZ. I presumed that he was looking for the ridgeline to open a little so we could find a suitable spot to wait until afternoon to be extracted. It was almost 0800 when we moved out.

After about one hundred yards, I could see the ridgeline begin to spread out a little. The trees were bigger and the slopes were not as steep. There was still thick brush on both sides of the trail that looked like some fifteen-foot bamboo mixed in with small trees, thick enough to walk through but good cover. I could see a higher outcropping out to the left that looked just like where we should go.

But, we began going downhill as the ridge began to slope away and down about three hundred meters to where our LZ should be. That scene would be burned in my visual memory for life. The end of the world was descending upon us; the terrifying noise of automatic gunfire from multiple locations tearing away vegetation and ripping into anything in the way was hell on earth.

"Ambush," I screamed as I dropped to the ground and sprayed the downhill slope with two magazines of ammo.

I unhooked a grenade, pulled the pin and heaved it, hugging the ground until a thunderous explosion rocked the ground.

I heard a painful "Aaaah" and discarded the double magazine.

As I crawled ahead like a frog on water, I reloaded, snapped the slide back on the rifle and let go. A round chambered and again I emptied a magazine. I didn't look up, left or right. I was only aware of Danny standing behind me saying, "I'm hit." He said it twice more, moaning. I threw my last grenade, crawled the ten feet back to where I had been and watched the vegetation tear away from the ground where the NVA fired at me. That shooting was drowned out by my grenade exploding. It felt like my ears and head were coming apart. Then, it was quiet, deathly quiet.

Danny was only about ten feet behind me, slumped against a big tree next to the trail. In a crouch I went to him. I shook him.

"Danny, you okay?"

There was no movement and my fingers on his neck felt no pulse. Danny was dead.

There was another tree almost opposite the one Danny was against. I went to it for cover.

The tree was on the same side as the NVA.

For the first time, I looked down the trail. Wise, in the lead, was trying to stand but he couldn't. His shoulder and the front of his chest was all blood. Behind him was Lieutenant Shinault, sitting with his head slumped down and facing the enemy. He looked fine. Behind him, and in front of me, was McAffe. He was on his back writhing around and holding his gut, in a puddle of blood.

"Lieutenant, you okay? Lieutenant, get down," I said. He didn't move.

To my right and down was a little opening, and if they were to come around to get to the trail, I could nail 'em. Tight against the tree, I could feel all the rounds rip into the tree on the other side. They heard me speak to the lieutenant. The tree saved my life. I stayed put.

In the few seconds of a lull, I radioed in.

"Sierra, this is Moleskin. We were ambushed, need assistance and medivac."

"Moleskin, this is Sierra, what is your location?"

Without fooling around with a reference point, I quickly looked at the map and gave them the exact location of our position. I was pretty sure the NVA knew where we were.

"Moleskin, how many wounded, over?"

"Sierra, let me survey the situation, over."

As it turns out, I have always remembered those exact words. As I took a step back away from the tree and clipped the handset to my harness, I began to crouch down to examine my team's condition. At that instant, an NVA soldier stepped onto the trail in a crouch opposite point man, Wise. He was about to move toward Wise and had his rifle at his hip and pointed at Wise. At the exact same instant, we were aware of each other.

The next two seconds in time seemed to span a minute. I swung my rifle around to my left and pulled the trigger and released eighteen rounds towards the enemy on the trail. At the same time, he swung around to his left to do the same thing. In the milli-seconds it took for my rounds to reach his torso, our eyes locked. His motion to turn was too late. He was beat. His eyes showed it. He knew it. He had such a look of imminent death.

At thirty feet, I could not miss. There was no look of panic or surprise on his face, it was the death mask of a man who was about to die. If I lived to be one hundred years old, I could never forget those eyes; I've seen those eyes and that face a multitude of times in the middle of the night when I sit up straight in a sweat with my heart pounding.

At the end of the milli-seconds when time stood still, his face contorted and shook as his arms flailed away and back. What was a man suddenly transformed into a scattered pile of dark red goo.

I felt nothing, no remorse, no sympathy, and no acknowledgement of the death before me. As I reloaded, I turned to find another target but there was none. He had stepped out on the trail alone. Maybe he thought they had us all down. He made a fatal error.

I heard movement and moaning below me. I took a grenade off Danny's harness and tossed it down and dove to the base of the tree. It was another deafening noise.

I saw movement to my right below the trail and fired off a spray of automatic fire. They somehow kept moving. I did a low crawl to McAffe. He begged for help and looked awful, his whole midsection looked like raw meat. I pressed two battle dressings onto what looked like the worst spot. He cried out in pain. There was no morphine to give him. I told him he would be fine and we'd be out of here soon. Help was coming. I think he knew better.

I got to the lieutenant and his ashen face stared straight ahead when I lifted his chin. The entire left side of his head was gone. It was like a cleaver came straight down and away. He would not need a battle dressing.

Wise was sitting, but moving in jerky motions and he had a huge hole in the left side of his neck. I took out my last battle dressing and just pushed it in the hole and lightly wound the cloth strips around his neck. I took two more dressings from his trouser pocket pouch and bandaged his left hand. He had three fingers missing. I pressed tightly on another dressing to his right leg, which had a bad wound.

The heavy pad of the dressing was quickly saturated with blood; I used the string from another dressing to tie a very tight knot around his leg above the wound. He was crying for "mama." He was crying for mama to help him. He was in shock and had no idea where he was. I stayed with Wise and radioed Sierra.

"Sierra, this is Moleskin. Be advised I have two KIAs and two seriously wounded. Need medivac ASAP, over."

"Moleskin, this is Colonel Asshole. You be advised to hold your position. There is a Bronco enroute to your position. A reactionary force will be there in four hours. Do you copy, over?"

"Roger, copy, be advised it will be too late for wounded. Cannot wait four hours. Need chopper now, over."

"This is Colonel Asshole. I order you to hold your position until reaction force can reach you."

I did not answer. The Colonel actually did order me to stay put, but I did not, I could not, I had to do all I could to keep them alive.

It was at that moment, in that little lull and after Colonel Asshole ordered me to hold position, I realized for the first time that I was alone in this. ALONE. Holy shit! It was the first time I switched gears from reacting as I was trained to thinking.

My first thought was that it appeared the NVA didn't know how many were still standing. Because I kept moving, they didn't know. What did they want? Did they want maps, radio or total annihilation? Why would they bother? Their known strategy was to hit and run, kill and maim all they can and get out. How many NVA were there? Were they regrouping?

The noise of a small airplane came to my ears. My head felt like it was splitting apart and my ears ached and were ringing so loudly, I was lucky to hear the plane. The rain had stopped but the cloud cover was almost complete, with openings here and there. The heat of the morning created a steam of evaporation resembling fog.

I reached up and switched frequencies. I could not make contact with the pilot. I switched back to my primary frequency and he was there. Sierra had given the pilot our frequency so they could monitor the transmissions.

I heard noise below and took a step away from Wise to move up the trail and slipped and fell in the NVA goo that was on the trail. I pushed Wise over and hit the deck as a burst of gunfire shattered the air and drowned out the approaching Bronco noises.

The NVA were too low and as they fired up, their rounds were tearing at the brush three feet over my head. The spotter plane flew nearly overhead but I missed giving him the mark-mark to indicate he was directly overhead. He made another circle around and I couldn't see him. I crawled up to McAffe and he was either passed out or dead. There was no time to check. This time I gave a mark-mark and asked where the enemy was from his view. It was just a few feet, maybe fifty to the west and downhill.

"I can't see your position and can't get too close to you."

He was referring to the pod-mounted rockets he had on each side under the wings. Those rockets were a kick-ass, kill-'em and scare 'em away weapon.

I gave another "mark-mark" and once again he circled around.

"Get down, fire in the hole," he told me. I was down, as down as I could get. It was at that moment I saw the little blue flower right next to my head. I had my left cheek on the dirt trail and that little, single blue flower was right there, as pretty as could be. I remember thinking, so this is where I die, next to a little blue flower.

The rocket hit. God damn did it hit. The impact nearly lifted me in the air and I am so thankful I had a finger in each ear. As it was, I was stunned. The rocket landed a little far down the hill. That was okay, any closer and I would have been toast. I grabbed my handset, told the pilot the shot was perfect and to check fire. I'd just have to take my chances without any more of that shit. Damn!

It was quiet again. Did I dare pretend they were dead or gone? No, I could not. I went up to the tree across from Danny again. Nothing. I laid down a full magazine and sprayed down the slope area just to let them know that all one hundred of us were still there.

I asked the pilot what he saw and his response to me was that I was not alone, he'd spotted four NVA through a break in the clouds and they were heading toward me but much further down the slope and at some distance. A hundred miles would have been a good distance.

I asked if there was any word on a chopper. He said no, and that he would harass the enemy all he could. There was soon a loud rocket explosion a "good distance" to the north and I went right down to Wise and said, "Come on, buddy, let's go for a walk."

I lifted him up over my shoulder in a fireman's carry just like I learned in boot camp. I had already slipped off his pack and taken both his grenades and his remaining battle dressings. He was heavy. I only got about thirty feet down the trail and had to put him down. I was almost to McAffe when a short burst of gunfire shocked me and nearly knocked me over. I thought I was hit but felt no pain. I returned the fire. Again, his angle of fire made the rounds hit too high and it was slightly behind me. I added another battle dressing to McAffe's wounds and sat him up. He was in wicked pain and awake again but totally oblivious to his surroundings. I knelt in front of him and pulled him up and over my shoulder. He cried in agony. Again, I had to step over and around the dead NVA and managed to get as far as Wise. Back on the ground, he passed out again.

They had no chance, I thought, but I had to get them to the LZ. When a chopper arrived, they must be put on right away.

I carried Wise again further down, as far as I could and put him down.

I radioed Sierra but it wasn't working; that's a bad time for the radio to have a dead battery, I thought. I would have to dig the spare out of my pack but I couldn't take the time just then. We needed to get away from the ambush site before the shit hit the fan again, maybe then we just might have a chance.

Off came my pack and it was left upright next to the trail. Back up the trail I went to get McAffe. He was worse, his agonizing screams were mere whimpers. But he was alive, at least for the moment. Carrying him went a little easier without my pack.

I continued to leap-frog the guys down the trail and finally saw an opening through the trees -- and daylight. I then noticed more breaks in the clouds and sun poking through. What a headache I had, my thirst was so bad I could hardly swallow and my heart was pounding out of my chest. I felt like I was going to pass out. We'll never make it, I thought. It was insane. I took a quick chug of water and just dropped the canteen. Back I went, about two more times.

We made the LZ and I laid out both Wise and McAffe next to the trail just before the opening in what little shade there was. That 250-300 meters from the ambush site to the LZ as shown on the map seemed like 250 miles. I tied another battle dressing around McAffe's lower abdomen and decided I could do no more. I had heard a helicopter a while ago but it didn't register. I heard it for sure on the LZ. There were two choppers way out there but I couldn't see them.

I hesitated. What about my training, I thought. What about the Marine Corps philosophy. A Marine never leaves a dead Marine on the battlefield. Oh, God. I filled my ammo pouches with magazines from Wise and McAffe. My choice was to go up two hundred and fifty meters into God knows what to get Danny, Shinault and my pack, or stay at the LZ and try to get the chopper in to get these guys out.

My decision was simple -- fight to keep the living alive and retrieve the dead later. The clouds clearing out seemed like a miracle and it was getting clearer by the minute. I could see the two choppers way out there and high. How could they not know where we were? I unbuttoned my left shirt pocket and took out my mirror, a shiny steel 3"x5" mirror, scratched up but still highly polished.

For the first time since I set foot in Nam, I was happy to have the sun shining on me. Angling the mirror in the direction of the chopper, I kept tilting it up and down to get his attention. Finally, the circling stopped and they headed toward me and began circling again, but much closer.

With no radio, they were reluctant to come in, not knowing what kind of reception they would receive. How could you blame them? I popped a smoke toward the middle of the LZ. It was hardly a good landing area, the opening looked like it was blasted open to make an emergency LZ. The flat top of the LZ and ridge was no more than twenty feet wide and was extremely steep on both sides. To go down either side would have to be done by rappelling. A chopper landing would be tricky, to say the least.

Wise rolled on his side to try to get up again. If he were to stand and fall, he could very easily topple over all the way down to God knows where. I rolled him over and he lay quietly. McAffe never moved but was breathing.

The smoke played out and I almost decided to go up after my pack when the lead chopper started his long approach while the gunship circled. He must have waited for the smoke to clear and knew what he had to do. I guided him in and he had a hard time. The wind uplift made the chopper sway and turn.

When he touched down, I ran to the gunner on my side and signaled him to come with me. He must have thought I was nuts and waved me off. I pointed to Wise and McAffe. The gunner took his headset off and I yelled that I needed help. He immediately unstrapped himself and jumped down to help me. We got both men onto the slick polished steel floor of the chopper and I jumped on.

The pilot took off his headset and I moved in close to him.

"Where are the others?" he asked.

"KIA" and I pointed up the hill.

He looked up to where I pointed. The trail head looked like a tunnel entrance, it went from sunlit brush to a dark opening visible for only a few feet. It looked evil.

As he attempted to lift off, I began to slide. By now, blood had smeared on the slick floor and was slippery. There was bad air, the rotors were having trouble with the turbulence. We went up and then plunged down and ahead. It looked like we were doomed but he picked up speed and swooped up in plenty of time. The tail rotor must have come very close to hitting the ground. I covered the guys the best I could to keep them from sliding. We became stable and away we went.

We landed on a small pad of steel mesh like at Quang Tri, beside a large metal building. Immediately upon landing, three medics in white rushed out, two of them grabbed me by the arms and forcefully slid me out of the chopper and onto a stretcher.

"No, not me," I yelled. "I'm not hit, get them."

I rolled off, reached on-board for my rifle while Wise and McAffe were slid off onto stretchers and whisked away. How could they still be alive? I jumped back on and into a smeared mass of blood covering the steel deck. I had a solid, crusty layer of drying blood from head to foot, literally, which was why they placed me on a stretcher.

God, how I felt so alone on the short ride down to the landing pad of Sierra - Vandergrift Air Base. I saluted the chopper crew and gave them a thumbs up. It was just before noon and a lifetime of shit had happened. I was drained but it would still be hours before I could strip the blood-hardened clothes off to shower.

I saw a Recon team assembled to my left and I started to walk toward them. A jeep intercepted me before I reached them. We recognized each other right away; he had been in "C" Company for a short while when I first got there before he left to go to the Comm. Command Center right there at Sierra. I didn't remember his name but he said, "Norm, was that you out there? We heard the whole thing. You're a fucking hero!" "Get in," he said, "the Colonel wants to see you."

I replied, "I'm going with those guys to get the lieutenant and Danny."

"Danny's dead?" he asked. I'd forgotten that the driver was a good friend of Danny's.

"Ya, he's dead." He looked down and paused.

"Get in, let's go," he replied.

I sat in the jeep and we took off for the Comm Center. I took the magazines out of my rifle and, as we hummed along on the steel mesh pad, I flung the magazines as far as I could, pointed the barrel up at the sky and pulled the trigger. The shot scared the driver.

"Jesus, Norm, what are you doing?"

I didn't answer. My rifle was cleared.

Colonel Asshole was pacing on the Comm. floor at the top of the stairs and across the room. I was on the second to top stair when he told me to halt.

"I don't want you on my floor, Marine," he barked.

"You make a habit of disobeying orders? Well, do you?"

Without waiting for a reply, he went on and on about something. His mouth moved and he was talking but I was in a trance, my head was pounding, my ears felt ready to burst and there was a loud ringing. I started to turn to go back down the stairs but the Jeep driver put both hands on my waist to steady me in position until Colonel Asshole finished talking.

I think he ended with, "And you'll hear more about this from your commanding officer."

I don't think I comprehended a word he said. Was I being laid out for disobeying an order?

What did I do wrong? On the way down the stairs, I had an awful sinking feeling that I should have gone back up that trail to try to get Danny and the lieutenant, but why? A Recon team was likely on their way to get them and two guys were still alive. Was I that bad a Marine? Should the end of this story have been retrieval of five dead Recon Marines on a jungle trail somewhere in I Corps near the DMZ in South Viet Nam? My mom wouldn't care where, she would always ask why. I think I fucked up bad.

My debriefing at G-2 was short. They just verified coordinates, number guess of NVA, uniforms, direction to LZ and that was it. They looked at my dried-blood body like a dead skunk in their living room.

Back at "C" Company, the first sergeant beckoned me to go upstairs to his living quarters. I had never been there. He was on his balcony when I was approaching. He knew where I was. I climbed the steep wooden exterior stairs and entered his two-room abode. The first thing I saw was a huge map of all of South Viet Nam on plywood mounted to the wall. Actually, it was many maps taped together. He looked me over head to toe while I leaned my rifle against the door jamb.

"You look like shit, son," he said in a stern but sympathetic way.

"Tell me what happened here at the map." He already had a pin on the last coordinates I gave.

"We heard all the transmissions at the Comm. Shack but tell me everything," he implored.

I asked for water and he obliged. I slugged down a fair amount and started at the beginning.

I was suddenly so tired I could hardly stand. When I finished, he almost looked like he could cry. I never saw that expression before.

"Get out of those clothes and take a shower, you stink."

"Yes, sir," I replied.

"You're a hell of a Marine, son. You did us proud. Git."

"Yes, sir" and down the stairs I went, wondering why he didn't scream and spit while asking me why I left two Marines on the battlefield. All he said was that another team was on their way out to retrieve Danny and the Lieutenant and our gear, if it was still there.

I did the slow walk down "C" Company. It was deserted, not a soul around. I hesitated in front of 3-C-1. It was deathly quiet. Next door, at 3-C-2, there was chatter inside and I dared not enter. I plopped down on a sandbag pile, leaned back against the sandbag wall of our hooch. With my rifle on my lap, I began to cry. I hung my head and cried like a little baby. It was uncontrollable. Danny is dead and I left him and Lt. Shinault on a jungle trail. They will hate me.

They heard me, I guess, and they all came piling out. They hoisted me up, hugged me, slapped me on the back and shook my hand. Their generous compliments gushed out. "Norm, you're the coolest dude in the Marine Corps." "How the fuck did you do it?" "We heard the whole thing until the end. What happened to your radio? We thought you were killed." "Norm says, stand by and let me survey the situation. Are you shittin' me?" "You had ice water in your veins." "How did you keep your cool?" "Everybody's talking about it. You're a fuckin' hero, man."

I was overwhelmed. "Jesus, get out of them duds, man." "Yeah, take 'em off out here." "You stink, man, take a shower." "Come on, let's help the man. We'll go to the showers with you."

And so it was. My head was spinning, trying to understand the reception my team and the first sergeant gave me compared to Colonel Asshole. Maybe I did the right thing after all. Maybe the Colonel had never been in combat and didn't understand about saving lives of fellow Marines versus following his order. I suppose he did have a point. The military has a basic premise that men follow orders as a matter of course. It is elemental to the whole structure of order and discipline of the military philosophy. I couldn't try to imagine how many thousands and thousands of good men through our history lost their lives because of bad orders.

I hit the rack right after evening chow. I went to sleep right away. The guys went over to another compound to grave registration, where they prepared bodies for the first phase of sending them home. They embalmed those they could, hosed them down and shipped them to Da Nang to do the rest. They saw Danny on the table. He had taken only one round in the upper stomach and they were told that a major artery was probably severed and he bled out internally quickly. The lieutenant's wound was pretty obvious.

The good news was that Wise and McAffe were still alive after surgery and if they survived another two days, they would be transported to the hospital ship off shore and from there they would be sent to Japan. We were told that if they could stay alive to make it to Japan, their chances for survival were excellent.

The following morning, we all went with the first sergeant to see our two fellow Marines. Wow! They looked like death warmed over and were so drugged up they weren't really conscious enough to recognize us. But they sure looked better than draped over my shoulder leaking blood all over me.

The shower I took late that day was the best I had ever had, or so it seemed at the time. When we returned to our hooch with the guys jabbering and asking Audie Murphy questions, my clothes were in a pile in the sand by our hooch. The next morning, they were gone. I never asked or cared where they went. But there were shitters being burned the next day.

The following day, the first sergeant told me of a battalion memorial service being planned for the lieutenant and Danny. He gave me instructions on what he wanted me to do. Their boots, rifles and covers (soft hats) were retrieved. I was to place their boots on the ground in front of their rifles, which would be stuck in the ground with fixed bayonets. Then I would place their covers on the top of the rifles.

The Padre said prayers and a couple of guys said a few words. The bugler did his thing and we all saluted at the proper time. We all wore our cleanest dirty uniforms. It was sad but the tribute was fitting and done right.

John went to supply and retrieved my pack. Why it was there will never be known. Damn. What a disgusting mess. As it turned out, the reason my radio crapped out was because it was riddled with bullet holes or shrapnel. What a story - radio man's life saved by his own radio. I'd buy that paper. I got a new pack and took the radio to the Comm. Shack for a full refund. They copied the serial number onto an official USMC form and threw the radio onto a pile of junk. I never even got a store credit slip. Cheap bastards.

Soon after I returned to the hooch in late afternoon, a second lieutenant wearing a crisp utility uniform came looking for me. He did the nervous introduction quickly. He had been a classmate of Lieutenant Shinault in high school. They joined the Marine Corps together, went to OTS (officer training school) together and came to Viet Nam at the same time. Both of them were assigned to the grunt unit I-9. But Lieutenant Shinault wanted to go to Recon to get his first lieutenant rank before his buddy. Geez, what a story. I could clearly see the guy was pretty shaken. I recognized him from the memorial service. He had been standing at attention next to our commanding officer and first sergeant. I invited him in where the guys were milling around cleaning rifles and writing letters.

Somewhere along the way, we had acquired a small round table and four rickety and rusty metal chairs that haven't been able to fold since they were in Korea. I had noticed that he carried a nylon bag when he arrived. He put the bag on the table and took out a bottle of Four Roses whiskey. Wow! He wouldn't say where he got it but it got everyone's attention. Out came all our tin cups and an extra cup for the lieutenant. We all sat around the table on the old chairs and some ammo boxes were piled up to sit on. The lieutenant poured out his story as we sipped on warm whiskey mixed with iodine-laced warm water. Man, it was good. Well, one must use an imagination once in a while and put yourself in that place and time. Yes, it was good whiskey. The lieutenant knew Shinault's mother; his father had died young.

So much had happened in the last couple of days -- it was chaotic for the base camp and half the time I was reliving the whole series of firefights, grenades and other events of May 7, 1969, so that I didn't think of the families of Danny and the lieutenant. They would have been notified by now and of course would be totally devastated. I felt terrible that it just hadn't occurred to me. Now I felt even more depressed.

The lieutenant talked on about Shinault's mom; Shinault was an only child and wanted to be a Marine like his father. He'd been a late-in-life child and his mom was in her 60s and suffered from a heart condition. She had taken the news terribly hard and had to be hospitalized. That's all he knew. The lieutenant was able to make radio contact from Da Nang and spoke with his own mother about Shinault.

The lieutenant asked me to tell him what happened and not to leave anything out. The guys were all ears, too, even though they had heard all the radio transmissions. But I hadn't yet filled in all the gaps.

I didn't want to talk about it, but it needed to be said. So, I went through the whole ordeal, blow by horrid blow. The lieutenant had tears in his eyes and hung his head when I got to the sad part about how his dear friend had died.

Without realizing the time, we had talked through chow and the bottle was empty. So were we, I guess. The lieutenant thanked me for telling him what had happened. He even wanted the coordinates of the ambush. I never did turn in the folded map I had carried and I used it as a reference when I was telling him. He wrote down 58°-15' latitude by 88°-10' longitude on the Cam Lo, Viet Nam quadrangle. He said he would get a copy of the map, mark the coordinates and keep it always to remember where his best friend died. It was a stone's throw from the DMZ. I was exhausted and went to sleep.

The next morning after chow, I wrote a letter home. It was short; I wrote that I would be pretty busy for a while and wouldn't be able to write. I told them not to worry, I was fine and would write as soon as I could. I just couldn't tell them anything about what had happened. My mom would have had a nervous breakdown for no good reason; it was bad enough for her as it was.

I sat and contemplated, for the first time, what families must be going through at home. I had thought about it, of course, and tried to be a little elusive in my letters home. But I hadn't really thought it through. I put myself in their place and realized how much their lives had changed since I arrived in Viet Nam six months ago. I had been so wrapped up in my team and missions and living day to day that I hadn't put myself in their place. I suddenly felt selfish. I probably would have been drafted anyway but I did volunteer. I was so proud to join the Marines that I never considered my family's feelings. I only thought they would be proud of me. Maybe they weren't. Maybe Norman, the eldest son, was causing more heartache. It wouldn't be the first time, for sure. I recalled my whining and bitching because I was 17 years old and didn't have my driver's license or a car. All my other friends had a car. I always had to bum a ride. Blah-blah-blah. I knew I couldn't get my license because I was taking a medicine that prevented me from driving. They thought I might have epilepsy. Testing every six months finally ruled that out and at eighteen I was cleared to drive. There were other times, as a kid, that I was less than a perfect child. Probably no more or no less than any other kid but after what I call the May 7 incident, I was pretty down on myself. It would be many, many years later before I would begin to realize the impact of the firefights, ambush, my friends dying, carrying friends out of the jungle and killing people had on my mental state of mind. I was melancholy, to say the least.

The first sergeant sent for me. That was almost always not good. One always tried to stay under the first sergeant's radar. But I had instantly become his favorite child, as the guys noted.

"Son," he said, "listen up. You have been written up for an award. The pilots in the choppers and Bronco, me, those who listened to the whole thing at the Comm. Shack and our CO (commanding officer) have submitted our testimony and you are being written up for the Congressional Medal of Honor."

"What," I replied, "are you talking about? Why? I was just doing my job. What was I supposed to do? What about the Colonel saying I disobeyed an order?"

"Never mind that," he said with disdain in his voice. "He was convinced to withdraw his hasty reaction to what you did out there."

"Oh," I said, "what does all this mean, sir?"

"It means you won't be going on any more patrols. The Marine Corps doesn't want you killed before you get your medal. You're a hero, son. Just think, Third Recon has two Medal of Honor heroes in one year."

I thought, who gives a crap about that. This isn't right. I wanted no part of all that. I wanted to leave right then.

"You will be working for me now," he added. "You'll live in the back room downstairs behind the office." And it went downhill from there. "You will be my administrative support chief." Yeah, I could see it coming. I'm going to be a fuckin' runner. An errand boy. A goddamned Recon errand boy. Just leave me with 3-C-2. I didn't say that but my face showed it.

"Sorry, son, but that's the way it's got to be. I'll move someone to 3-C-2. In the meantime, you move up here. You will be the go-between with G-2 and the team being fragged." I was being demoted to nothing more than a Company Clerk with less responsibility. Some reward to look forward to.

"You will make sure they get all the maps and gear they need."

Oh, good. I'm a quartermaster and mule, too, I thought. I wonder if I'll get a bicycle with a basket and a little bell to ring. I can deliver mail and sell ice cream on the weekends. This is bullshit, I thought.

CHAPTER 19

The guys took the news about the same as I did. Then the teasing started. They started saying what I was thinking. "Hey, Norm, when you get moved would you please bring us a bucket of ice for cocktails later. Oh, and don't forget the cigars again today." Ha-ha-ha. They could see that I saw no humor in it at all and they began to commiserate with me. John said he would plead our case to the first sergeant but I knew he'd get his ass kicked out the door about fifteen seconds into his plea for mercy.

I settled into my routine of humiliating drudgery. The days were long and boring. And then, after about four days, I got a message from G-2 for a mission for "C" Company. It was 3-C-2's turn to go out. It was a suck-ass mission that was out quite far and right on the big red line that was the demarcation of the DMZ. Sierra would be the relay station. We had been up in that area known to be occupied by the enemy before. Besides, so much fighting had been there that half the jungle was blown away. I was told that a major operation was being planned and they needed more information. Further, I wasn't there to question them, only to get the orders, debriefing sheets and maps.

"That is all, Lance Corporal."

"Yes, sir," was all I could say. Shit.

I stopped by our office to check our mail with the company clerk. I thought I'd take it down to my old team with all the maps and stuff. The clerk said I was just stalling and he was right. So, I gathered up all the stuff to leave and pimples, the clerk, said, "Oh, by the way, First Sergeant is at sick bay. He's got gout again and won't be back for a few days."

"Yeah, okay," I said, and off I went to deliver the bad news.

After a great deal of discussion and looking at the map, we talked about our team situation. I had forgotten that John was really short on time. His 13 months were just about up. The mission at hand would, for sure, be his last time out to the Pointless Forest. Juan was a short-timer, Nick was gone, Bart was short and had another month to go. Doc thought he would be called back to the hospital ship at any time. He wasn't looking forward to it.

So, there were John, Bart, Juan and Doc for the mission. Because of the terrain and hostile activity expected, the guys said they should take a "law" with them. The "law" was a kick-ass powerful big cylinder weapon carried with a sling. A high explosive round was put in the cylinder and placed on one's shoulder. A magnetic trigger set off the round toward the target. We needed to remember to stay away from the back of a law. There was a back blast that would probably kill a human. It was an all-business weapon primarily used by the grunts, but in a situation like the mission planned, it was a good decision to take one.

Extra weight and four guys were not a good combination. And, who would carry the heavy radio and battery along with the radio operator's duties? We all looked at each other and then they all looked at me.

"Yup," I said, "deal me in." John said he would talk to the first sergeant.

"He's in sick bay for two or three days," I told them.

"Oh," John said with a grin, "I guess I'll have to decide myself."

That led to a discussion about whether or not it would be disobeying an order. It seemed like I was just recently in that discussion. We decided that, technically, there was no direct order given me, just general instructions on my new post. Besides, orders from G-2 on this mission must be considered. The decision was cast. This would be John's and my last mission.

God help us.

I still had my pack and harness and all my gear. We prepared well and I slept on my old Civil War cot one more time.

Loaded down and with nerves on edge, we waited just a short time before hearing the familiar chopper coming our way. It cut a straight course through the morning air and landed near us.

It was hot already and, with some apprehension but with a familiar ease, 3-C-2 slid our butts down on the steel deck of the chopper. With our legs and feet dangling over the side of the open slick, we lifted off toward harm's way. Each of us were already there in our minds. I was focused on what the LZ might look like. Before landing and five hundred feet in the air, it would be a long look at the terrain below. How open was it? Which side of the LZ would provide the most cover? Did anyone see movement anywhere on the ground?

It was a go. The chopper went in fast and low. It was tree-top low to keep visibility from the ground at a minimum. Suddenly it looked like we would have a big problem, as it appeared broken tree trunks would prevent a landing. John had to decide quickly whether or not to abort. We were not taking on fire and we saw no movement. Could the chopper get low enough to jump?

There were no throw-out rope ladders available in Viet Nam like there were in years to come. The chopper hovered. The obstacles on the ground weren't broken trees, they were large termite mounds. I had heard about them but had never seen them. The mounds were seven to eight feet tall, taller than a man. They were about six feet wide and tapered somewhat at the top, not unlike a pyramid. They were as hard as a tree. The mounds were really dried mud that the termites had digested to build their castle home.

John jumped and we immediately followed. There was no time to waste. It was a long jump, about ten feet. With a heavy pack and rifle, it seemed like jumping off a roof. I hit the ground and did a half-roll before my pack stopped me. I quickly readjusted everything and headed for the tree line behind Juan.

Shit, Doc didn't get up. When I glanced back to check, I had the radio handset in my hand in the process of waving off the chopper. It was up and away in a flash. Juan and I ran back to Doc. He was getting up but had apparently rolled his left ankle and we half-carried him to the tree line while he tried to hobble along.

There was no evacuation rope on the chopper. John said to release the chopper to get him out of the area. We had to deal with Doc the best we could. It was quiet. We all kneeled down around Doc without moving. Normally we'd get on the move quickly. Juan stood up and moved about fifty feet away to watch and listen. Doc was wincing. He wiggled out of his pack, turned around on his knees and retrieved an ace bandage. I was amazed. I had no idea he carried one. It was hard getting his boot on over the bandage but it worked. We were good to go. It was shitty terrain, all vines, too open and no big canopy trees. We didn't cross a trail all day and Doc's ankle was getting worse. He didn't dare take his boot off.

A steady light rain started to fall late in the day. We found a nice knoll to occupy at dark and settled in. The rain increased and the fog was dense. I actually felt pretty safe. By morning, Doc couldn't put weight on his leg without a lot of pain. With the continuing rain and fog, we sat tight all day. After dark we decided to stay put. It was shit luck that we didn't move. Finally, the rain and fog subsided somewhat by dawn. A can of peaches and a swig of iodine water with a salt horse-tablet was a great breakfast.

One more day of this crap and John and I would be done with the jungle. John would go home and I would be a gopher again. As much as I feared every mission, at least I was an integral part of a solid team doing a job very few people in the world would ever understand or appreciate.

Hell, very few people would even be capable of doing what we did. We were good. We must be, we were all still alive. It wasn't until later that I would think back on being a Recon Marine and realize just how much confidence in myself and pride in who I was would affect my personality and work ethic. In civilian life, it seemed to me that I was able to tackle difficult jobs and solve problems a little better than most of my peers. I seemed to be able to address life's pitfalls better and certainly I would appreciate the fragility of life with greater understanding than most.

John decided that he and Bart would make two or three expanding circles around our position to see what was going on. I stayed with the radio with Doc and Juan. That sounded reasonable. They would be back in about four hours. Our legs were cramped so we moved around a little to stretch our leg muscles. We were starting to dry off a little. It looked odd to see steam coming off five wet Marines. It was getting steam bath hot. They waited a while to get dried off and avoid leaving a telltale vapor trail. I remember we quietly chuckled at the thought of those two guys creeping through the jungle giving smoke signals to the enemy.

Doc took some aspirin. I didn't know he carried aspirin, either. I also found out Doc was far from being a crybaby. Not once did he whine and complain. His reply to "How ya doin', Doc?" was always, "It's not bad, I'm good to go, just a little slow." He fit in.

If anything were to happen, our rendezvous point would be west of the LZ where we doctored Doc. We sat in silence to listen. I did not radio in our plan. That was something that was never done. The main function of the hourly sit-reps was to give our position and verify all was secure. That would soon change.

This was the first time in all the missions, in all kinds of weather and situations, where we stayed in one spot for a day and a half. Of course, those long-range jobbies out at Uncle Ho's Trail and a couple of times deep in the DMZ no-man's-land, we sat tight, but not these missions where our job was to cover a large area in five days.

The air was dense, heavy with moisture and still – unnervingly still.

Then, the crashing, piercing, air-shattering noise of automatic gun fire tore through my ears. In a second, my stomach clenched, my heart started to pound and the adrenaline overflowed. I rolled. My pack was heavy dead weight on my back, pressing down on me. My rifle was pointed toward the threat. It was hard to breathe. It was deathly quiet.

On our knees, we stared ahead and then at each other. What the fuck was that? There was still no noise. All I could think about was my last mission ambush. John and Bart would be toast! Juan and I helped Doc to his feet and he said he was good to go.

Amazing. In just a few feet, we stepped onto a well-worn trail. We were so close. Doc hung back a little. Juan and I crept up that dark ribbon of dirt separating thick jungle vines and tall gangly trees with twisted thin trunks. Around a turn and a little uphill, there was a small protected opening beside the trail. I ventured forward with my rifle raised and finger on the trigger. The safety switch was off.

Here was the source of automatic fire. There was lots of blood. The red pools were soaking into the dirt. There were no bodies, no moans of pain or any sign of John and Bart. What the hell was going on? Blood trails disappeared into the thick underbrush. The jungle had swallowed all noise, all but my pounding heart.

We stood dumfounded. The only scenario that made sense was that John and Bart initiated contact from the trail. Why? Both sides must have been surprised. Who knows? I did know that we needed to stay put just off the trail and wait. It couldn't be over. And wait we did. After some time, we heard movement. With raised rifle and poised to release an eighteen-round magazine at the enemy, around the corner on the trail came John. He actually looked happy. Bart was soon to follow. Bart said to keep moving, we were being followed by several NVA. They would be moving slow, wary of a trap. We were less concerned and moved as quickly as Doc would allow. He did great and we did not dally. The NVA would not be ahead of us. They were all the other way, I pretended. All I could envision was the horror of recent memories.

Please, dear God, not again, please.

The trail was going too far south and we needed to head more northwest. We had to abandon the trail. We were trying to keep track of where we were and stopped to check the maps. John took out his compass and I gave my map to Bart while I radioed in where I hoped we were. I conveyed to the relay station our position and destination.

Another team was being inserted on the edge of the DMZ and were to cover a large area to our northeast. Between us, which would be about two miles, was an anticipated stronghold that we all were to verify. We may have found an edge of it. There would have been no fear of the two teams running into each other because of a buffer in between where the suspected NVA would be. Our mission -- penetrate to the enemy position, observe, follow the edge of their positions, withdraw and report. Between Doc's ankle, the weather and open terrain, we found the enemy the hard way. Our chopper would be available by the time we got to the LZ. There was always the danger of going right by a small LZ. We had done it before and had to circle back but never with God-knows how many of those little gook bastards on our tail.

Doc was hurting but he toughed it out. Juan hung back as usual and kept putting two fingers to his eyes when we looked at him. He could see them, or at least movement. There was no shooting. With the LZ just ahead, I drew a sigh of relief. And then I remembered, this was our insertion LZ. Doc got hurt because the chopper couldn't land. There's no way they could get us out of here on a rope. We would be picked off like balloons at the County Fair.

We reached the opening at a fast walk and Doc held his own. He had to cross the LZ to get to the other side and keep open space between us and the gooks. The small opening now looked like ten football fields. It was probably only about one hundred and fifty feet wide. We started to jog our way across. Bart, in his point position, stopped at one of the largest termite mounds, jerked off his pack, and we passed him.

He quickly fished out the detonation cords, wrapped it around the mound, set up the charge and moved on to two more termite castles.

The NVA opened up on us, more particularly Bart. He heaved his pack on, lit the fuses and ran like hell to the nearest termite mound. The shooting wasn't very accurate because they weren't quite close enough.

The blasts were deafening and pieces of the mounds flew everywhere. We hit the deck and were littered with debris. By that time, Bart made a mad dash for a termite mound closer to us away from the middle of the LZ. No choppers yet. John asked me if I could throw a grenade far enough to reach a certain dead tree that had to come out to get a chopper in. I thought so. At the count of three, we took a hop and a skip. We each chucked a grenade at the tree. Mine landed about five feet right and John hit the damned thing. It fell straight down. That tree never had a chance. It was history. A chopper could land but none in sight.

I called out to the pilot on the radio but no reply. The gooks had settled in and we exchanged fire. It was like the Civil War, the Union Army on one side, the Confederates on the other and a field in between. Thank the Lord for those termite mounds. They were being shredded.

Juan uncorked his law and buzzed a round into the gooks. Who knows what the results were but they were spreading out. I had the handset to talk to the relay station about our chopper so I wasn't shooting. I was on one knee and John was standing next to me. Juan and Doc were behind another mound about ten feet away and Bart had his own private mound on the other side of me about twenty feet away. It was getting so I couldn't hear a damned thing.

Suddenly, I heard a pilot calling. I answered and heard him ask for a smoke and sit-rep. He didn't like my answer. I don't know why, but I stood up. I think it was to get a better look at the sky for the chopper. Right away, I spotted them coming in from the east. It was not right and I yelled for him to bank right and circle.

Christ, just our luck. It was a big old CH-46. The gunship was high above and circling. We only had three smoke cannisters between us. I threw a green smoke out but not far and told the pilot we were right behind the smoke and the gooks were on the other side of the LZ in the tree line.

The chopper backed off and the gunship made his first run. He fired two rockets and a shitload of fifty caliber. It was then that I killed the last two gooks that I know of. To our right, two gooks stepped out into a very narrow opening. They were obviously trying to flank our position to get behind us. They both went down in a heap with heads flung back. I flipped in another magazine and called the chopper.

For some reason, John rested his right arm on my shoulder and was firing short bursts. The pilot told me to stop yelling. I couldn't even hear myself talk. My left ear felt blown. The pain was incredible. I pushed John off and looked up to find my pilot. The gunship made another run and I signaled Doc to throw a smoke. Juan was shooting his M-79 round after round as fast as he could.

Right after the gunship passed, the CH-46 came in perpendicular, low and fast. As the hydraulic tailgate was going down we made a run for it. John stayed with Doc and we used the big chopper for cover.

Juan threw his smoke out in the opening between us and the gooks. It helped screen us a little. We were all in.

We slowly started to lift up and, as we did, something big hit the tailgate and practically took us out. The tailgate was still moving but crooked and couldn't close. The chopper dropped a little and crept up again. I thought we were in our coffin. All that was left to do was die. That chopper was rockin'. The gunner on our side was non-stop. The other gunner took the machine gun off the mount, pushed the ammo box and belt across the aisle and set up in a window. We all took positions in the other two windows and unloaded everything we had. The thud-thud-thud of rounds hitting the fuselage lessened as we gained altitude. We went up, tilting back to front and side to side. It was like being in an unbalanced washing machine. The shooting stopped. We banked one more time and headed for home. We would live. The entire floor was littered with spent casings. Simultaneously, like some rehearsed movie, we just dropped our rifles and slipped and slid toward each other for big bear hugs. That included the two gunners and crew chief.

I could hardly hear a thing, my head was throbbing, my left ear was draining. But I had a huge smile and there were no holes in me for blood to run out. We were all alive.

The next day we would learn that John and Bart stumbled onto a trail we were next to, only they found it some distance to the west. They followed it, went practically right by us and heard voices. They crept forward and observed four NVA soldiers in an overnight bivouac area next to the trail. Instead of coming back to us, they attempted to quickly dispatch the NVA and maybe get a prisoner or info off the bodies. The plan failed. John said he thought they only got two of them and the other two returned fire. John and Bart stepped behind trees on the trail and the gooks beat feet, taking their buddies with them. John decided they should follow and intercept the gooks but there were other NVA on their way to look for their buddies. Both John and Bart realized they fucked up and turned back to meet up with us. They realized they did the wrong thing but they knew this was our last mission and they were sure they could get a wounded prisoner. That lapse of judgment, which seems small, nearly got us all killed.

The jungle is unforgiving. You can never make a mistake, ever. Death follows failure around like a deserted puppy dog. He who makes the fewest mistakes lives. He who is lax and fails but only once must die. Warriors in the jungle make those rules, not politicians or dumb ass generals. War is the only chess game where the pawns make the rules and move to their own position. The pawns develop the strategy to stay alive on the board. At the end of the game, when the last pawn is standing, the King Generals declare victory, give themselves a medal and promotion, light a cigar and call Walter Cronkite with a news report. The President nods his approval and clinks glasses of smooth bourbon with his Cabinet. The pawns stay on the table, set up for a new game and are on their own to fight for another win, over and over again. The games must continue until the politicians get tired of playing.

We slipped, slid and staggered off the broken tailgate and onto the tarmac. A sharp salute to the pilots and crew sent them on their way to the repair shop. We needed repairs, too. We were beat. We unloaded our ammo at the dump. Old Sgt. Grumpass wasn't there but a short, black snake was nailed to the plywood wall. Maybe the old boy was napping. Leave him be, said we. Doc was dropped off at the corpsman's shack, G-2 was done with and my radio turned in, and we plodded our way to the showers with towel, soap and truck-tire flip flops.

It was done. My jungle adventures were over. Maybe the first sergeant would say, "Son, I'm going to make you a corporal and give you a team - all new guys. You be careful, now. The DMZ is a dangerous place. Good luck." Nah. He wouldn't do that. Yet, on the other hand, this was Viet Nam.

CHAPTER 20

It was time to write home and color in more squares on my short-timer's calendar. The letter home was still a little elusive. Years later, my dad told me that when I wrote to say I wouldn't be writing for a while and not to worry, that all was well, he knew then that all was far from well and that's when he began to be really concerned. Dad was in Africa and France during World War II. One cannot bullshit a bullshitter, as they say.

I remember the next day being very laid back, even restful. It was reflective and I felt like a seasoned veteran. After morning chow, we walked down the lane of Charlie Company together, our metal trays, cups and silverware clanging. We sounded like a herd of cows headed to the barn at night to be milked. That brought back childhood memories. I wonder whatever happened to the old cowbells of yesteryear. They were probably on an old wooden beam somewhere in the barn. Maybe they are still hanging on some big old cow, but I doubt it.

3-C-1 was a new batch of guys that were cobbled together from another company. They were out on a mission somewhere. One of the guys had a beach umbrella that he dragged back from R&R. Who would think to bring an umbrella back to Viet Nam? That made about as much sense as bringing back a box of ribbon candy.

Actually, maybe the umbrella made sense after all. There was a semi-circle of sandbags three layers high between our hooches. I got the umbrella which was kept just inside the door of 3-C-1 and jammed it in the pile of sand just so. We sat on the sandbags in the shade. It was about 8 am and already it was nearly one hundred degrees in the shade. We had a thermometer on our hooch. I wish I had taken a picture of our little outdoor patio. The only trouble was it was pretty close to our piss tube so it smelled a mite like the old outhouse.

We were talking about how close we came to dying the day before and listening to John's story about why he and Bart decided to open up on the gooks. We were analyzing the logic of their actions when we were shocked to see the first sergeant walking down the lane towards us.

"Hey, boys," he said with a somewhat cheerful greeting.

At least it seemed cheerful to us, coming from "The Man."

"You got room for me there?" he asked. We quickly scooted over to make room for the big guy. By now, we loved him like a father. But we could sense he was not there to wait with us for the ice cream truck to come along.

"Boys," he said, "You three have given Recon a good name. You have carried on our tradition. You're good Marines and I'm sorry we can't all stay together but life goes on."

And on and on he went for a while about how he loved Recon and how proud he was. He certainly had our attention and he seemed a little melancholy. He shared with us that he was hearing gossip from up the ladder, which meant Battalion Commander, that President Nixon was going to start withdrawing troops and Third Recon would be pulled out and sent to Okinawa.

He then started to talk about training. He picked our brains on how to prepare Recon Marines for jungle warfare. We had gone through Camp Pendleton where it was far from jungle environment. He talked about World War II and what the Marines went through on all the jungle islands to defeat the Japanese.

How can you possibly train Marines to do a job unless you go to a similar environment, he asked.

We told him the only way to train Recon how to do their job, say in a jungle, is to have instructors who have been there, like us. We learned from each other. All the things we did that were so unique about Reconnaissance and jungle warfare, we learned from those who had done it before us. It was impossible to anticipate what you would and could encounter unless you've been there.

"Sir, does that mean you might want us to be instructors when we get to Okinawa?" I asked, hoping he would jump on it.

"Nope," he replied, "Just askin'."

"VanCor, your orders came in yesterday," the first sergeant went on, "you have been approved for R&R in Hong Kong. When you return, I have orders for you to report to Headquarters Battalion over near Dong Ha. Do you know how to run one of those radio vans they mentioned in the orders, a TSC-15 van?"

"Yes, sir," I sadly replied.

"Good, you are required to be able to do that because that's your new job. What the fuck is a TSC-15 van?"

I explained that it was the most powerful radio the Marine Corps had. It was powered by a generator and the transmitting power was unlimited. If there were another van on the moon, you could communicate with it. It was in a box-type square metal thing with a door and a huge antenna. There was room inside for one operator and a chair. Two people could fit inside, but certainly not comfortably.

"No shit," he said in amazement, "Who on the moon would you need to talk to?"

"Well, the whole idea, sir, is that you can patch generals and important people together so they can talk from different parts of the world."

"I'll be god-damned," he said in amazement, "that ain't good when those sons of bitches can all talk together at once."

So, my fate was sealed. I would be leaving Recon. I really didn't know how I felt. For sure I didn't want to go back out in that jungle again. On the other hand, being a Recon Marine was the first thing I ever did in my life that I was really good at. I was physically a tough dude and my mental state was as sharp as a razor. It seemed second nature to me. I reacted well to stress and, God forbid, a firefight. I was good, damned good. I found something I was superior at and I wanted to keep it. Instead, I was going to sit in a cramped metal box listening to the bigwigs brag about how successful their war was going. Are you shittin' me?

I was given a secret clearance when I finished radio school in San Diego. Actually, the secret clearance process was pretty impressive. The FBI actually does go out to interview people and do a thorough background check. They interviewed my parents, school principal, chief of police, neighbors and even medical background. My family and neighbors were wondering what was going on with all the questions but I wrote to them to explain what it was about. When I heard about all the mysterious questions by FBI agents, I didn't even know what was going on until I went to ask the school gunnery sergeant.

The first sergeant went on to tell John that he, too, had orders. He would be leaving for home the next week and would be mustered out of the Marine Corps in San Diego, his hometown. He would have less than six months left of his enlistment so they wouldn't send him to a duty station for such a short time.

And Bart, he was also pretty short. He had only about three weeks left of his thirteen-month duty in Viet Nam. The first sergeant said he would try to keep him in base camp but couldn't promise as he was short on men. As it turned out, Bart did go out again twice. They formed another team and he was promoted to corporal and team leader. Both missions were successful and he left Viet Nam in one piece.

The first sergeant excused himself and walked away. He had a purpose for everything he did. He deserved our respect.

So, with the news to digest, we chatted about our new assignments. We then started to talk about our time together at 3-C-2. We had our shit together and we hated to give that up but we had our fill of missions, constantly alert to stay alive. We compared ourselves to the WWII hell they went through.

In the final analysis, we couldn't figure out what it was all for. What was it that we contributed that would win this war? What was the real purpose? That old, long-bearded bastard was still alive. What was the DMZ for? The North Vietnamese sent men down across the DMZ. Recon found them, we killed them and they killed us. So, the North would send more and on and on it went. Was it to see who would run out of men first? It was craziness. It was a merry-go-round of death.

And then we talked about our missions and inevitably the jungle itself. The more we talked, the more we realized how much we all feared and hated the jungle. From the moment we ran across the LZ away from the chopper and entered the edge of the dark, other world, until we stepped back into the sunlight of a small opening and boarded a chopper, we were in its grip. It was a world of danger, fraught with the unseen and unheard creatures that bit, chewed, sucked blood, and threatened every step in an evil, sunless hole. The jungle was alive. It was a life unto itself. Add to that the unseen enemy with dark skin, slanted eyes and light feet who lurked within the vines and underbrush, ready to thrust a knife, throw a grenade or empty a magazine of bullets that tear and puncture flesh and bone, leaving the jungle to claim and devour the body. The floor of the jungle was litter, just dead material that snakes, centipedes, ants, Asian worms and spiders crawled through to sting and bite and inject venom for the next meal.

The vines and canopy interlocked like a woven impenetrable prison cell. The leaves hung overlapping to block out the sun. The water was undrinkable. It was a haven for parasites, leeches, water snakes and mud creatures. Giant spiders wove their webs overhead to catch any flying creature that ventured near. There was no wind, no moving air. It was stifling. Trapped heat made steam on a good day and fog when it rained. Rain fell through the canopy of leaves as through a strainer. The rain created life on the ground and all dead things were eaten or left to rot. It was hard to breathe and nearly impossible to walk except with effort. The smell was closed in, moldy and pungent. It was organic, like a pile of compost all closed in. There was a human desire to keep moving. Sitting would mean that the creatures would find you. The mosquitoes, insects and all things that crawled found us and fed upon us. When we left, we had welts, bite marks, swelling, rashes, jungle rot feet and nightmares.

The dead bodies we rolled off the trail and covered in floor litter were devoured in short order. The jungle claimed everything. It rotted clothes, rusted metal and broke down flesh. Its vile breath of death whispered our names every night. The invisible "Keep out - danger ahead - no trespassing" signs were ignored. We had to enter its grip and fight to be released. The jungle is a very primal place.

The scientists, researchers, National Geographic and nature TV shows all love the jungle. Only the brave and the adventurous dare enter. Its dangers are well documented. Once penetrated, the dark world of Lucifer will dominate your body and soul. It is not a place for the faint of heart or the unsuspecting and naïve. The jungle is unforgiving and harsh. It is a place for death to nourish itself. The jungle would occupy its own place somewhere deep in my brain for a lifetime. It would never leave. It always comes out at night to make me remember and think about and overruns all other thoughts until it conquers my brain. Only then will I awaken, cold but wet with sweat, to recognize the beast within. Once awake, the jungle withdraws to the deep recesses of my brain and awaits the next opportunity to attack my memory and remind me in dreams that it is alive. It will always be alive.

The more we talked about the jungle that day, the more we realized that it was good we were done. We did our part, maybe even more than our share. I became strong. I endured. I killed people. I've saved lives and upheld the traditions of the U.S. Marine Corps. I gave my best and gained confidence and respect for myself and all those like me who had the guts to enter the jungle and search for the enemy. I learned to adapt - improvise - overcome.

I needed more cigarettes, so we walked over to the MASH unit area to a haphazard PX in a small hooch. All they sold were cigarettes and toiletries. I wished it was a liquor store. There was a gook man giving haircuts so I got something that resembled a haircut from him. It was cheap. We hit the showers and afterward I took a salt horse pill, washed it down with iodine muddy water and took a nap before evening chow.

One thing most war observers overlooked in all the drama of battles and intrigue over the mechanics of war was the fly boys. The helicopter pilots and crew, F-14 Phantoms, Bronco spotter plane pilots were all a tough breed. Special emphasis should be placed on the chopper pilots and crew. They had guts and devotion to their mission. Not only with Recon, but their willingness to dive into an intense firefight to drop off water and ammo and take out the wounded and dead was truly heroic. I knew they were our salvation from certain death repeatedly. In WWII men had no choppers and continually moved forward, taking with them supply chains, portable tent hospitals and other necessities of the war. These things were "in the rear," as they said. In Viet Nam the front was also the rear, the head was the tail and the general was the ass. We all know the ass is never in the front.

The chopper pilots and crew amazingly found a small opening in the jungle way out in the DMZ somewhere that was sometimes half hidden in fog and rain. On the radio with me, they were to the point. They wanted wind information so we popped a smoke. They wanted precise direction of enemy fire and obstacles in landing. Never once did they hesitate to come in after us or say, "Geez, you fellas should fight it out or outrun 'em. It's kinda foggy, guys, we'll try to get back out tomorrow."

Nope, they came every time. They came in fast, low and straight with the whole chopper rocking from the gunner putting out those 50-caliber bullets by the hundreds. We were on the run and jumped aboard and before our butts hit the deck we were in the air. Maneuvering to go straight up was hard. The choppers can't get loft with any speed so it all takes time. But, they did it. They all knew the dangers.

I've spoken to pilots who have told me after I've thanked them that they would do what they do all day long but they could never switch places with me. They were never overlooked or taken for granted by Recon. Quite frequently, we had Army Warrant Officers pilot, co-pilot and crew come out for us. We particularly liked them. They were young, full of piss and vinegar and they all had big balls. The Army slicks were a little smaller with less room and open, with no doors. But there was enough room for three guys on one side and two on the other with our legs dangling over the side. They were like bees. They would dart in, pick us up and dart out. They had all the armament but it was just more efficient. The CH-46, two top-rotor choppers with the hydraulic tail ramp, were Marine Corps issue and usually piloted by Majors. They were a little older and had a wife and kids at home. They were good but just a little more hesitant. There were frequent issues with the CH-46 about enough landing space or a hot LZ and other problems and they were slower and harder to maneuver. There was more than once when we got away with what should have been disaster. Bullets hitting the fuselage of those babies was like hail on a tin roof. All it takes is one bullet to hit a hydraulic line or rotor coupling and we would have inherited a large green metal coffin.

When the pilots came in to get me on that very narrow and steep LZ after the ambush, they needed every bit of skill they could muster to get us out alive. The wind shear was wicked and I thought we were going down.

During all the hoopla of everyone writing me up for the Medal of Honor, the first sergeant asked about the pilots and we agreed that I would write a description of what they did and the decisions they made. Without radio communication, it took guts to commit to a run in to save us. Those two guys I carried out would certainly never have lived if we had to wait for a reactionary force to come in. Hell, for that matter, I wouldn't have made it either. The gooks would have left a pile of bodies. Many U.S. Infantry admittedly did some pretty uncalled-for atrocities in Viet Nam. But the NVA and Viet Cong were no better and most experts agree that they were worse. Their handling of prisoners was similar to the Japanese in WWII. When given the chance and enough time, the gooks had a ritual of maiming our dead. Their signature calling card was cutting off the dead soldier's balls and stuffing them in his mouth. We hated those slant-eyed little yellow bastards.

The Phantoms, as they were called, was the Air Force contribution to our needs in Recon. They were the fixed wing jets (F-14) that supported Recon and Infantry. It was a single pilot that was occasionally called in to kick ass on a large number of NVA. Sometimes we observed the enemy, took notes, disappeared and reported our findings to G-2. Other times, depending on whether or not they were on the move, we would call in for fixed wing. I remember one time in particular.

We penetrated the jungle to a particular spot where the enemy was suspected of having a staging area to move men south. Looking at the map, it was fairly predictable where they would be and we were right. There must have been at least fifty to seventy-five NVA preparing to make a coordinated move. It was scary. We used binoculars and dared get no closer. They were in a fairly open valley and we were higher up.

We intentionally climbed up a fairly high ridge to get a good view and, bam, there they were. The NVA were in a pretty tight area and seemed to be preparing to move. It was a perfect opportunity to call in fixed wing. After the request, it had to be okayed by the latrine masters and only then would come the order to scramble a jet. They were coming from Da Nang, over 90 miles away, so we waited. The coordinates I gave were checked and double checked. I switched frequencies and waited.

The pilot came up on the net to verify coordinates. I gave him our position and terrain info. All of a sudden we could hear him. We expected him from the south but he was coming in from the east, putting us on the ridge between him and the gooks. That was not good. The jet noise got louder and louder and then we could see him starting his run. It was a steep dive that would put him right over us. The last thing he said was, "Get down and hold your breath."

He came screaming in and dropped a large napalm cannister. If I could, I would have had poopers all over my pants. That cannister was tumbling end over end and it looked like it was headed right between my eyes. As he came roaring by us overhead, he was so low I could see him clearly and even see rivets on the plane. He pulled up and banked hard right over the valley. The gooks had zero chance to react.

We did as he instructed and, as the napalm hit its target, hell on earth enveloped the land. A fireball of gigantic proportions billowed up in a boiling mass of hot gases of orange and black. The blast rocked the earth and sucked all the oxygen into the inferno as it rose to what seemed to be two hundred feet in the air. We literally could not breathe for a few seconds. The sight and sound were so incredible, we could only stare at the holocaust unfolding before us. In our stupor, we didn't notice that the pilot had made a large turn and was calling me. I told him his aim was perfect.

"I'm coming in at this time," he announced.

Holy shit, he was headed straight down and following the valley straight south to north, perpendicular to his first run and where we first expected him. Once again, the horrific engine screamed downward and as he started to pull up, another cannister began its end over end float down to a fiery burning death to all survivors of the first assault.

As he circled around, I gave him the all clear, job well done and a thanks from Recon.

"Roger," he said, "Always glad to help you boys out. What do you have for a body count?"

Yes, of course, there's always a body count. That day I gave him a count of one hundred for his list and the Walter Cronkite nightly news.

Looking down at the valley was mind-boggling. It was Satan's lair. It was a huge desolate wasteland of burning earth and trees, charred body parts, scorched earth and thick greasy black smoke with the stench of death. Small fires burned and the crackling of it was the only sound in the valley of the shadow of death. My God, what just happened? We wondered how many American lives were saved by killing those NVA soldiers. It took all of twenty minutes to execute the entire event and move on. There was no point in going down there. It was a solemn place on earth that may never be walked on again. I switched frequencies, radioed in a quick situation report and we continued our mission for two more days without seeing any more NVA. We had seen enough.

Somewhere in the grand scheme of life on earth, God must grant us peace. Intervals between wars are short. In that interval, we invest in newer, more efficient and powerful ways to kill people. The bombs are bigger, the planes are faster and stronger and the politics gets angrier and clouded with self-righteousness. The strong shall survive at least until someone is stronger. Vengeance is mine, sayeth the general. Here, sayeth the wise old Senator, have more men and more bombs. Go away to play. Reports. We want reports, we sayeth. Fuck you, all of you, and the horse you rode in on.

CHAPTER 21

The trip to Da Nang to catch a plane to Hong Kong was bittersweet. Yes, I wanted to get out for a while. But, Hong Kong? I wanted Hawaii but only the married guys got that. My only other choice was Singapore. What's the difference?

I met up with my cousin Ronnie while waiting for a plane. He was in the Army, stationed in Da Nang. He was in teletype and supply. Without guys like Ronnie to move supplies, we would have been in big trouble. The logistics of efficiently supplying a war effort is a fascinating study. The monumental burden to consider everything needed to support troops is mind-boggling.

It was a very secure area. He had a beautiful room, white clean sheets on his bunk, and maid service for making the bed, washing the clothes and other cool stuff. Good for him. I was pleased he was where he was.

We had only a short time to visit. I told him I'd try to look him up on my return. They had special cabs at the airport in Hong Kong waiting for us. I didn't realize it but it was just a scam. The cab drivers were really just handlers. He took me to my hotel and told me to have the hotel call him and he would take me anywhere I wanted, any time. So, I checked in and went for a walk. The streets were teeming with people.

I was definitely alone. No one, and I mean no one, spoke English. There were no burger joints or any visible signage that would give me a clue as to what was inside the storefront. I was hungry but didn't know where to go. I made it back to the hotel and had them call Hop Sing. He drove me to a sort of club. Now we were making progress. I ordered a scotch on the rocks and began to relax. Hop Sing spoke with a Mama San and then introduced us. I said I wanted steak but oh, no, they have better. You like. Yeah, okay. After another scotch, I was really hungry. They delivered a bowl of what looked like chop suey. Mixed in the mess were chunks of white-brown meat that I hoped was chicken. It looked more like Old Sergeant Shitbird's snake chunks that he always had nailed to his shack. I ate some and pushed it away. Out came another scotch and Mama San with a sweet young thing who obediently sat down beside me. Great. Just what I needed. She also got through to me that the little beauty queen was mine. Mama San presented my bill. I had exchanged greenbacks for Hong Kong currency. I paid Mama San what seemed like a lot of money for cheap, watered down scotch, a bowl of chop suey with pieces of snake or cat and a teenage whore. Naturally she didn't speak a word of English and kept her head down like she was a bad girl caught behind the barn with little Jonny.

I called Mama San over and told her, no girl. I want money back. I go now. I found myself talking like Tonto on the Lone Ranger show. She was waving no but I took back a handful of their money and got up and left. Little beauty queen stayed with Mama San. It was tempting to take sweet thing and I wasn't practicing to be a priest, but she was more than a tad young. I shouldn't have read that brochure about VD they gave us. I had the name of the hotel written down so I got a cab back. A long, hot shower felt heavenly. Crisp white sheets felt good too. There was no artillery or mortar fire but I fell asleep anyway. It was good.

Naturally, Hop Sing took me to a tailor shop. The material was mostly silk and beautiful. They measured me head to toe and I picked out colors and patterns that suited me. I ordered two suits and several shirts and trousers. I left with a slip. They would be ready in two days. I was in Hong Kong for five days. Next, my handler took me to the port to the duty-free retail stores for unsuspecting naïve tourists like me. I must have stood out like brass balls on a wooden monkey.

I bought a bunch of dumb stuff for my family. At the time, I agonized over all the purchases. I wanted to get just the right special thing for my mom, dad, sister and brother. I bought my mom a white coral necklace and bracelet thing, although I had only seen my mom wear a necklace maybe twice before at a wedding. I couldn't ever remember her wearing a bracelet before. But I just had to have it. It was pretty big. A year later she showed it to me because I hadn't seen her with it on and I had forgotten what it looked like. Good grief, what could I have been thinking. She must have thought I had stolen it from a medicine man from deep in the Congo.

After I had been home from Viet Nam for a few months, I tried on my new threads. Yikes! Not only did nothing fit, but it wasn't even close. Why didn't someone tell me not to buy clothes on R&R. All those beautiful silk clothes were too small. The measurements were accurate enough, but I had gained back the weight I had lost in Viet Nam. My dad was quite pleased with his new suits. They all fit him perfectly. All was well.

I went out to a good-looking restaurant in downtown Hong Kong for dinner. Again, no English. I resorted to pointing to something on the menu that looked good. I must have made a good choice because scrawny little Chinaman said, "Ah, number one, Joe like."

"That's good, Joe wants another scotch, no water, just scotch," I said as I pointed and tried to act out what I wanted.

He came back with a handleless cup with some warm yellow stuff in it. I motioned for him to take his warm piss away. There was a little fella in a sort of cubicle where there were four or five bottles of booze and some wine and saki. I reached over and took down a glass, filled it with Cutty Sark and gave up on the ice. The little guy didn't seem offended. "Ah, number one, Joe."

It wasn't long before my meal came out. I couldn't believe it. I swear this is true. It was some sort of stew or soup in a thin greasy liquid. There were greens and little bitty ears of corn with roughly chopped bamboo, I think. But the best part was in the middle. Sticking out of the witch's broth were two chicken feet and legs. Its claws were curled and stiff. Whatever bird belonged to those feet could have been in the bottom of the bowl or on someone else's table but it would forever be a mystery. That waiter looked so proud of the whole thing. He bowed and had the biggest yellow-toothed grin I ever saw. Right then I wished I had a tin of pound cake and some canned peaches. Good old C-rations. My friend with the yellow teeth looked on in bewilderment as I pushed the sloppy mess away from me, swallowed the rest of the scotch and threw some of their money on the table. It must have been enough or more than enough because he didn't follow me out jabbering in Hong Kong talk.

I found a sort of bakery and bought some sweet rolls which were really good. The rolls plus some of what looked like cookies held me over. I did a little sightseeing by cab but not much else. I was kinda bummed. I wanted to get back before John left for home so as soon as I paid the tailor and made shipping arrangements, I caught a plane back to Da Nang. I cut my R&R short. Who does that? I looked up Ronnie and stayed overnight with him. There was an extra bed because his roommate was shacked up with his girlfriend in the whorehouse across the street. We sat on the balcony of his hotel home and sipped some good scotch. And we went out for a great steak dinner. I should have stayed with him instead of the Hong Kong disaster trip.

The next day Ronnie found me a helicopter ride to somewhere and I made a lucky connection to Quang Tri on a CH-46. I was back where I belonged. And then I remembered that I wouldn't be there long. I had orders waiting for Headquarters Co. My TSC-15 van awaited my arrival. I hoped I could remember how to run one of those rigs. We didn't have much training and they were complicated.

The first sergeant caught me as I walked by his office and quarters at the head of "C" Company. He kidded me a little. He was glad I got a rest and hoped I hadn't caught some disease from the little ladies. I told him I was pretty certain I had not. He informed me that my write-ups for the pilots went through and they would be awarded a fitting decoration. That was good. They deserved it. Then he told me he got paperwork back from General Shit-for-Brains that the MOH write-up was denied. Apparently, there was some rule in the Marine Corps that there must be two documented accounts on the ground to witness the actions. Since the two with me were in shock and could not provide witness to the event, they intended to award me the Navy Cross, the second highest individual combat medal for heroism. And the South Vietnamese honcho in the area offered a document to award me with their highest honor, the "Vietnamese Cross of Gallantry." The old bird wasn't pleased that I just said, "Thanks, that's good." I guess he expected me to act more favorably and appreciatively to such honors. The whole thing still hadn't sunk in about that part. What I did have on my mind was that Danny and Lieutenant Shinault were dead. I just didn't get the medals part. I didn't want medals soaked with their blood.

The first sergeant did have good news. His inquiry through Command about Wise and McAffe came back positive. They were both in Japan and doing well. Both were expected to go stateside in a few weeks. Now that's more like good news.

Tomorrow I would leave for Headquarters Company but tonight we would celebrate our time together with a bottle of Four Roses I smuggled in my bag. Good old iodine water and whiskey. Life was good. It would be my last night on the Civil War cot that I never got used to. I discovered that there was absolutely no conceivable position one could lie that did not make your body ache in the morning. I should have slept on sandbags. But in a perverted sort of way I would miss my old cot, blood-stained from the unknown soldier and all.

Our little soiree with the bottle of Four Roses was bittersweet. Our talk was matter-of-fact and somewhat emotional. We had been through a lot together. The realization of our parting of ways was confusing to us. Who could ever believe what we had done and seen? What would it matter? Would we keep in touch? What would we do with our lives? How could we ever have friends when they would seem shallow and insignificant? Do you have to have done what we did to be in some club? Are we better or worse than our peers back home? Would our peers of the future think we are better or worse people than them? We must keep in contact. We knew we wouldn't. We knew we wouldn't tell anyone about our missions and our experiences. They wouldn't understand at all. They wouldn't give a damn anyway.

After morning chow and after a big ooh-rah and goodbyes, I had my orders, a seabag with all the uniforms the Marine Corps issued to me and a handbag of useless treasures. The Company Cluck drove me away from 3-C-2. We weren't going far to Headquarters Co., maybe five miles, but it was like driving away from home and family. I guess my war was over. No more missions in that dark jungle fraught with fear, things that crawled and lurking death. I made it out alive and should be happy.

My friend, pimple face, the Company Clerk, drove me away and we went in silence. He kept looking at me and finally started to tell me things that surprised me. He blurted out a series of complimentary words. He admired me, the First Sergeant liked me, he knows he couldn't do what I did, that's why he was just a clerk. He was proud to be a part of such a team as Charlie Company.

I felt small. I never gave him a chance to be a part of us. He was just always a company clerk, no face, no one you'd talk to. Heck, I didn't even know he had a name. I felt very humble. He was a real person with feelings who cared. He was doing his job just like I was doing mine. We were both Recon Marines.

I smiled and shook hands with Fred. "Thanks for everything, Fred. You kept everything running smooth. Take care of the old man on the second floor." I gave Corporal Fred a respectful salute and, with my seabag, handbag and an empty M-14, I walked into the office of Headquarters Battalion, Third Marine Division, and announced myself.

The old gunny was a typical Company gunny. I figured him to be about 83 years old. Between the ages of 60 and 70, while he was a staff sergeant, he remained at USMC Parris Island inside a jar of pickle juice. He was a wrinkly, gnarly, gravel-voiced old coot who spit at life. It was easy to see that he had had an anger implant at some point. He wore starched utilities with pressed trousers and a half-ass shine on his boots. He rattled on for some time about how this ain't Recon.

"We have discipline here," he started. "Don't forget, you are a Marine and you're expected to look and act like one around here. If you understand that, we'll get along fine; if you don't, you'll be in a world of shit like you've never seen before. Do you understand, Lance Corporal?

"Roger, copy, Gunny," I answered smartly.

"Yeah, well, okay and I don't need a smart ass, either. What I need is a body to run a TSC-15 van. Do you think you could just maybe know how to do that?"

I said I thought I'd remember. We only had one training class on it but I'd figure it out. His speech continued on about how he doesn't need maybe's and promises. "This is Headquarters Battalion and you are a radio operator 2531 and you'd damned well better know how to run a fuckin' radio. This ain't that Recon bunch, you've got to show me what you can do. We've got responsibilities here. We run this whole fuckin' shit hole war and you'd better get your shit together and keep it together. I ain't gonna put up with any shenanigans here and no pot smokin' mutha fuckin' green ass punks are gonna get by with shit on my watch. This ain't Recon here so get squared away and stay that way. You've got radio watch tomorrow 0800-1200 hours and TSC-15 van review and start-up with Sergeant Walker at 1400 hours. You got that?"

Yes, sir.

So that was my new life, I guess. The barking gunny was quite a character. I'd find out just how much of a character before too long. Writing home to give my new address and the news of my transfer would be comforting to my mom, I knew. I played that up. I've been in Viet Nam almost eleven months now and my short-time calendar was really starting to show some color.

My new living arrangements took me by surprise. A mere five miles or so from Recon Battalion base camp and a world apart in living conditions. I entered a wood structure barracks. There were about twelve cots in the room. It was larger than my old 3-C-2 digs and seemed brighter and more airy. It was the same old canvas cots but I had a pillow, at least. When I walked into the barracks with my gear, I plopped my rifle on a nearby empty cot and was bashfully greeted by three guys who seemed to scurry apart when I entered.

I must explain here an important lack of knowledge or naivete in me. Brought up in the Berkshire hills of western Massachusetts and graduating from a school in a small town, Southington, Connecticut, in the late 1950s to mid-1960s, little country bumpkin wasn't very sophisticated on certain things. For example, I never saw a black man until I was 16 years old and living in Connecticut. There was one black kid in our whole school, my class. We became pretty good friends and did a lot together. I had never seen a combination lock until my sophomore year in school. When we moved and I went to high school, I didn't know how to open my locker. I'd never seen such a strange contraption. I didn't even know why there would be a lock there. Finally, the whole notion of pot and joints and roaches and rolling weed into cigarettes was never thought of. I was never exposed to it or heard anything about it in our little Puritan bubble of that time period. It changed quickly and drastically.

These guys scurried suspiciously apart like they got caught behind the barn doing a nasty. I thought nothing of it but noticed the cigarette smoke smelled quite odd. They walked out and I unpacked and went for a walk to check out the area. There was no sense taking my rifle because I had no bullets and the area was quite secure. The whole camp was a sprawled-out affair with no perimeter fence. There was a very large motor pool, artillery unit, large helicopter pad, crane helicopters, medical dispensary and sick bay, lots of specialty shacks, including two large Comm. hooches with signs above the door and all. The mess hall was huge. I went inside to look around and had a coffee. At the Recon mess hall, it was locked except for meals. There were several barracks and even a club. The door was locked. I wondered what the "Club" sign really meant. The office was almost out of walking range and I noticed a lot of guys using jeeps to go about their business. It was a little like a mini town. I met all the guys in the "barracks." They were okay but pretty stand-offish.

The Club finally opened and, like magic, about thirty guys were in line. The line was for beer - cold beer. There was a generator out back and a window a/c unit stuck through the wall. It was cold in there. It was uncomfortably cold. The air was cold but still humid. There were about ten tables with six chairs at each. Everyone bought two beers at a time. There were even two or three choices of beer. Luckily, Miller beer was a choice so I stuck with my old standby. I sat with a group and introduced myself as a transfer from Recon. They seemed uninterested and their talk was shallow and two or three at a time left for a while and came back. I had thought they were using the popular piss tubes outside the club.

This went on for three or four days. My days were filled by field checking radios, cleaning and minor repair. It was mundane and boring. More paperwork on transfer, shots and assignment had me to the office quite a bit. I got my first assignment to fire up the TSC-15 van that afternoon. I was patching a general in Saigon and a general in Okinawa with some general in Washington, D.C. at the Pentagon. I got the code book and routing numbers. I beat feet over to my new toy. There was a secure area in the Comm. area off limits to most personnel. It was the main Comm. Command Center for Quang Tri. Within the secure area were two TSC-15 vans. In between the two vans was a rickety wooden lean-to protecting an even more rickety generator. If the generator didn't run, I was out of business. My mechanics skills were very low. That poor generator was given another chance. My belief was that General Patton had abandoned said generator beside the road while fighting his way through Sicily and Italy. The Italian government had no use for such a derelict so they gave it to the Marine Corps and now it was mine.

The gas and oil were good to go and with two five-gallon cans of reserve gas, all looked ready. It fired up just as it had for that lance corporal all those years ago in Sicily. It sounded like old Mr. Howes' antique Farm-All tractor he used to spread manure and scare the cows with. But it smoothed out and ran like Uncle Walter's old wood splitter. Inside the van, I flipped switches up and down, pushed buttons and input codes. A bunch of lights blinked on and a noise like an F-14 making a bomb run made the van come alive. It was all normal. In ten minutes, I would begin my radio procedure talk to get all the mucky-mucks happy and feeling wildly important. I looked forward to listening to all the high-level secret stuff they would discuss.

It turned out to be a bitch session on supplies and shipping schedules. I learned that the conversations weren't much above that level. I guess it kept the generals busy. After about a week of the high-level secret clearance patching and being shunned by everybody around me, I found out why and things came to a head in a big, big way.

I was sitting alone in the cold, clammy club, drinking Miller beer two at a time and smoking Lucky Strike C-ration cigarettes with brown age spots on the wrapper when a guy pulled up a chair and sat next to me.

"Hi, I'm Norm. I haven't seen you in here before."

"Yeah, I know who you are," he replied and added, "I've been here but not a whole lot. Look, I don't know you or know why you're here but you seem like an okay guy."

"Thanks," I replied, "I'm new here."

He interrupted me with a clear message, "Shut up and listen. Whoever the fuck you are, they think you are CID (Criminal Investigation Department) and your ass is grass."

"What's CID?" I asked. I genuinely did not know.

"Look, don't play dumb. All I'm gonna say is that you and the Gunny, right over there, will be leaving together tonight. They've figured it out."

"They who?" I interrupted.

"Those guys right over there," and he pointed to four or five guys sitting at the table in the corner. One or two of them were paying rather close attention to me.

"When you leave this place, you and the Gunny will be fragged.

It's none of my business. I just thought you'd want to know. If I were you, I'd go straighten this out with them."

And, with that, he got up and left the club. I finished my cigarette and last beer, got up and walked straight to that corner table.

"Can I sit down?" Without an answer, I sat down and said, "So what's up? I was just told you guys have a bone to pick with me. What's your fuckin' beef with me? I haven't done jack shit to you guys. I don't even know you."

"You don't, do you?" said a little dude with a big attitude. "We think you might know us more than you say and we sure as hell know your game. Recon, my ass, you're CID. You know it. We know it. We're all done playin' games with you motherfucks."

"I don't have any idea what you're talking about. I just transferred from Recon and you guys have an attitude and some bullshit story about CID, whatever that is," I pleaded. "You've gotta tell me more."

"Okay, big shot, we've noticed you don't like a little weed now and then."

He explained what CID was. A CID agent was embedded with them and was discovered. Apparently CID agents were similar to, or part of, the Military Police, but with more authority and drama. They were more like detectives or the FBI. They were secretly embedded in a unit with high rates of drug use and other illegal activity, to bust the ringleaders and stop the illegal practices. They took him away after that and a week later, I showed up. They assumed I was a replacement and since I wasn't into pot, it added to their theory. I was tried and convicted. And, since they hated Gunny Bark, they planned to get us together outside and roll a grenade our way at the right moment. Voila! Problem solved.

One must remember that in Viet Nam, life wasn't worth much and getting away with something was pretty easy. Homicide detectives were hard to come by. A good friend of mine from my younger school years was from a quiet farm family. After high school he joined the Army. He went to Viet Nam and two weeks later he was shot in the back and killed by friendly fire. Imagine what his parents thought. Phil's father was one of my Boy Scout leaders.

It was all so innocent back then. There was no crime, no fights and little controversy. It was a town of farmers. It was all milk and honey. Phil was strong like an ox, quiet, yet aggressive on the athletic field. He was always chosen first when picking sides for the softball teams at recess. Who would want to kill Phil? Throughout the years since leaving the Marine Corps, I've visited Phil's grave many times and almost every Memorial Day. He lies next to his mom and dad in our little Ashfield cemetery in a quiet corner next to a fragrant lilac stand that offers magnificence every spring.

I was mixed up in craziness. I left the discipline, togetherness and respect of Recon and came to a pit of biting mongrels, drug-crazed zombies. I was confused and unsure of my safety. I was at a table of Marines staring at me with despicable hate in their eyes and tongues of sharp threats.

"So, what do you want from me?" I knew I needed to stall for a little time to think. Things were quickly getting out of hand and I had some tough hombres bearing down on me.

"How about a little toke? You say you're not CID. Prove it. CID don't do pot. What do you say, hot shot?"

My answer was swift and sure. "Okay. I've never had pot but if you guys need some sort of proof, I'll smoke your pot, say tomorrow night?"

"Nice try, Recon. No dice. Tonight and right now," was their answer.

It was late and I was tired and filled with four or five Miller beers. "Okay," I said, "so we'll smoke pot. Where?"

"You smoke pot with me," said Amazon. I didn't know anyone or care to know their names so I just nicknamed the gang or called them Joe. So, the huge guy stood up and stretched out to exaggerate his bulk like a mating baboon would do to attract a female. I didn't laugh at Amazon but I was nervous. He didn't intimidate me but I wasn't exactly in control of my situation either.

On our way out of the club, Gunny Bark gave me and Amazon the evil eye. If he only knew. Our little walk seemed further than necessary to smoke a joint. Onward we went across the gravel road through a very dark night illuminated not by street lights or a friendly lamp in a friendly window but by the brilliance of every star in the Milky Way. It was just the night we loved when my beloved 3-C-2 was deep in a remote jungle lair. We could get our bearings from the stars for our next day's travel and enjoy the starlight to observe our surroundings. One always misses what one doesn't have.

That night, on the gravel road, my travel was uncertain, an undesirable and foolish mission of stupidity. I found myself standing next to Amazon in front of my primary TSC-15 van. I was perplexed. It was a secure area. There should have been a guard or a sign or something to keep us out.

"In here," he announced with some authority.

"What's wrong with right here, there's no one around," I countered.

"In here," he insisted.

So, I turned the handle, opened the door and stepped inside with the hulk. He latched the door closed. It was hot and stuffy. It was very close quarters. I began to think immediately that this was something I did not foresee. This wasn't about smoking pot, it was about sending a message to higher-ups. Don't send anymore CIDs because they will end up dead like that last asshole you sent. It seemed clear to me that my options were very limited. I put my right hand on the snap of my knife sheath. If I unsnapped it, he would surely hear it and he would immediately thrust his knife blade deep in my gut or chest. It was absolute pitch black. Sweat beads ran down my face. My shirt was already wet. It was getting harder to even breathe in that tiny space.

He moved his arms. I leaned backward and managed a small step away to throw him off balance if I could. It was too dark to catch any movement at all. The silence was quickly interrupted by the strike of a match. Light burst out from the match and sulfur filled my nostrils. He lit a joint and took a deep drag. All the while, his glare bore through me. He passed me the joint. I told myself it was just like a cigarette, so why not?

The pungent smoke was inhaled deep into my lungs. I began to cough and fling sweat from my face. More coughing made Amazon smile as he filled his lungs with more smoke. The haze was visible from the burning end of the joint, and the outline of his face was like looking through fog at a ghost. The solitary light from the burning rolled pot provided just enough light to see both his hands and be fairly certain I would live through this. Once more the shrinking joint was passed between us. I was gagging for lack of air and the inside of my little van was filled with smoke. Amazon turned slightly, turned the door lever up and flung open the door with a mighty heave.

He quickly stepped out and looked up at the sky. One step forward and I was in the doorway. Smoke poured out. I could breathe and the cool air caressed my face. I stepped out and looked up also. I saw the totality of the universe seemingly for the first time. The enormity of it all left me speechless. I stared up in dumbfounded amazement.

"So, what do you think now, Recon?"

My confidence soared and in a euphoric voice I blurted out some profanity and asked if he and his prick buddies were satisfied. I was pissed and half-laughing at the same time. What a goof. I was definitely not in control of my faculties. My thought process somehow got rewired. Amazon seemed like a pretty decent dude after all. I think the door of the van was left open that night. We walked back to the club crunching the gravel on the road while talking nonsense about nonsensical things. The guys all seemed happy at the club. They bought me more beer. They talked and my head bobbled from one to the other. My plaster smile must have amused them. I must have made it back to the barracks because I awoke the next morning in my bunk.

I was accepted into the tribe. But I didn't like the tribe any more than I did before. I just couldn't figure out how they all got to the state they were in. It was as if they were cloned from the same robot. These wasted derelicts weren't good enough to burn shitters in Recon. No wonder the gunny was a barker. He had a platoon of buffoons.

The days ticked by and letters from home were my sanctuary from the asylum that had entrapped me. Almost every day there were generals here in Nam who just had to talk to some mucky muck somewhere. The redheaded sergeant seemed to always be working on one or the other of the vans while I listened to the bigwigs gossip and pat each other's fanny with compliments.

There was talk about General Westmoreland's reports. It was all so phony and contrived. I began to think this whole war was a promotion opportunity for a handful of generals. It seemed the President was poised to begin troop withdrawals. It was a campaign promise that must be fulfilled. They were probably running low on body bags.

I drove over to Recon on a day off. The first sergeant was in his room so I knocked on the door. He seemed really happy to see me and talked to me like I was a real person. There were few left at 3-C-2. Charlie Company was down two teams and what guys were left were dispersed here and there.

He didn't confide in me, of course, but he did confirm that things were winding down. Recon was preparing or at least beginning the tactical process to evacuate Quang Tri. Third Recon would soon be transferred to Okinawa, its home base. Now I wish I could be there. I told the first sergeant about the misfits of Headquarters Battalion but I didn't say anything about my pot adventure. I did tell him about all the drug use and laziness of the whole place. He said he knew. He then talked as if he were speaking to himself in a distant voice. He let me know this wasn't his first war. Headquarters always seemed to attract the derelicts of the Corps. It was mostly guys unfit for combat or meaningful duty. There were exceptions, of course, but Headquarters was definitely not the pride of the Corps.

Viet Nam was different, though, he added. It was a different mentality. Nam was a mistake, an unwinnable mess started by President Kennedy and made worse by Johnson and now Nixon. The young Marines were less trained and motivated. They were two years and out bodies, not the Marine Corps he knew. We were the exception, he emphasized. He asked, to no one but his alter self, "Why do you think we took the best? Why do you think we did not tolerate any pot or booze?" He stopped there after he seemed to come to and realized that I was still there. "Thanks for stopping by, son. Stay away from all that stuff. You're Recon. Stay that way. Take care of yourself and do well.' With that, I left, never to see the old boy again.

I did hear from him again about twenty-five years later. After I was divorced from my wife, I rented an apartment and lived alone. One weekend day I answered the phone and heard a voice that was immediately recognizable. His booming voice sprung me to my feet. "Hello, son, this is First Sergeant George Saxton, remember me?"

My quick response was clear. "Of course I do, yes sir. It's good to hear your voice. Where are you?"

"I retired in San Diego. I live in one of those complexes for old people," he responded. "Listen to me, son, the reason I am calling is to tell you that I've spoken to a friend of mine, a retired general who lives here in this place. He's a good man. We talked about you and he agrees you should have been awarded the Medal of Honor. He thinks we can fix it. We're going to ask the Marine Corps to re-open your file and award you the Medal of Honor like they should have done in the first place. Remember Captain Randall, our company commander? Well, he's got Parkinson's disease and he's all used up, ain't worth a shit anymore. But I think I can get him to sign some papers. If I have to hold his hand to do it, I will. I've been in touch with Third Recon Battalion Association. Are you a member? Anyway, they will write a supporting letter. Now, listen to me, I want you to get hold of your U.S. Senator, the best - that Lieberman guy - and tell him what we're doing and tell him to help us out. You follow?" That was the first time he took a breath and paused so I just replied, "Yes, sir."

"Good. Now this might take some time but those bastards better do what's right."

"Yes, sir."

We did some loose chit-chat for a minute or two. He asked what I was doing with my life, kids and so forth. Apparently, his health was pretty fragile. He said he wasn't planning any more than a week in advance, don't make sense, he said.

So, with that, we ended our conversation and we never spoke again. The Marine Corps did open my file again but stuck by their strict rule of boots on the ground as witnesses. Senator Lieberman said he would support the cause but it was for naught. The good thing about that whole deal was that I discovered there was an Association. I made contact, became a member and was put in contact with John, Juan and Bart. No one ever knew what happened to Nick. We all thought he probably moved back to Puerto Rico, where he was born. We never found him.

About two years later, First Sergeant George M. Saxton died. I was sad but knew I was a better Marine and person because of him. He was a good man and an honorable Marine. If he asked, I would have followed him into the valley of the shadow of death to cover his back. I swear I would have done that for him. He really was "The Man."

CHAPTER 22

The days and weeks dragged by at Headquarters Battalion. Rumors still floated around about going home early. It didn't matter. It seemed like nothing mattered. My whole existence seemed to be in a vacuum with no escape. I was abandoned and alone with repetitive days and nights, each as meaningless as the last.

As crazy as it sounds, I missed my team. I'm not sure if we ever did anything to advance the progress of winning the war or stop the dreaded spread of Communism the politicians were so worried about. I wasn't even sure if I knew what war was anymore. The whole notion of the hit and run tactics with no vision for the end game completely mystified us. To all of us who were in firefights, who killed the enemy, spied on them and called in bomb runs, the purpose was elusive. Our internal goal, and it seemed the goal of all infantry and Recon, was to live through the next firefight and keep yourself and your comrades alive for the next day.

I inhaled deeply. The smoke filled my lungs. I held my breath to keep the smoke in and gradually exhaled smoke so I could drag on the joint again. I was alone, sitting on some sand bags, deep in thought. Pot was so incredibly easy to get. For one U.S. dollar you got ten beautifully wrapped joints, all uniformly sized and neatly packaged in a cellophane wrapper.

I kept my stash under a particular sand bag that was outside and against our barracks. There was no one around and there would be no conferences that required a TSC-15 van. I was getting high. I didn't know why nor did I even think about it. I wasn't happy and I wasn't sad. I guess I was in a melancholy mood. I preferred to be alone. I didn't care about or trust anyone around me. I thought about home. I missed my family. I didn't really miss my friends any more. None of them ever wrote to me, not even once. I got a short letter from my second cousin, Christine, but that's only because I wrote to her and asked her to send me a picture of herself in the snow. I always really liked her. Her letter was short and she sent me a winter picture of her grandmother's trailer.

I was pretty certain I would live to get home. My mood was more reflective of what I was missing in life. I was stuck in a wretched and desolate wasteland that only the local villagers could love. And even the poor locals never smiled. They all went about their business with the water buffalos, toiling in the rice paddies. Their homes were of pieces of plywood and other discarded materials scrounged from the American dumps we seemed to have everywhere.

Many of the locals were displaced due to the fighting over the years. There were two generations of them affected by war. The French were here before us and Chinese before them. The locals didn't like us or hate us. They simply tolerated us. They used us, stole from us, and even harbored the Viet Cong to kill us if there was an advantage for them. Young boys accompanied their sisters, some not yet teenagers, to prostitute themselves for a C-ration meal. They sold us rubber-soled flip-flops, their daughters and wives, pot and information about Viet Cong movements.

Their cemeteries were bombed, run over by tanks and artillery. Idiot Americans would shoot their water buffalo for sport. Their water buffalo was like our tractors. They were their greatest asset, sometimes their only real possession. We took their land for our bases and walked into their little villages to search for Viet Cong. We spilled their rice sacks on the ground, held guns to papa-san's head to get information by force and sometimes burned homes because we thought they were harboring the Viet Cong enemy.

After all that, we asked them to be thankful we were there to save them from the threat of Ho Chi Minh's Communism politics. They didn't seem to care much at all about politics. The locals had no friends, no peace and no life, only turmoil, hate, disease and intruders. Through all that, Americans fought and spilled blood in death to save them all. How ironic.

There was a so-called roach left of my marijuana cigarette so I flicked it out into the sand. I sat there in a semi-stupor and listened and looked around. There was no sound, not even a bird, a helicopter or artillery. My surroundings were flat, dirty and a little sad. To the left a short distance away was a mostly destroyed cemetery. A mounded crypt had been turned into a French bunker two decades ago.

My thoughts wandered to my own hometown in Western Massachusetts. Our beautiful little cemetery where I will rest someday had lush green grass, lilac bushes and grand oak and maple trees providing shade. Birds of all kinds were on duty all day to sing for the deceased. No foreign force has ever trampled our sacred ground or displaced our lives. Our families were all intact and living without fear. I thought of our sophisticated life at home with all the comforts and security of a civilized society. How good it would be to have all Americans sit here with me to observe what the South Vietnamese people have in contrast to their own lives of riches. If a Vietnamese farmer cut his finger and it got infected, he probably would have died. Their bellies were extended by the time they were twenty years old because of the water they had to drink. All the women started chewing betel nut by age fifteen and by age twenty their teeth were black and falling out from the effects of the tobacco-like substance in betel nut. The men smoked a pretend tobacco in a pipe, cigarettes, or the cigarettes we give them in exchange for screwing their youngest daughters.

I must say emphatically that I was celibate my entire time in Viet Nam, not because of some moral or religious obligation. No, it was simpler and more private. All the guys that took great pleasure in screwing every girl in the village had VD or gonorrhea. Their sense of pride and integrity was sacrificed. I was no minister of righteous conduct and all fire and brimstone jargon. Nor was I a better-than-thou kind of guy. Just do what you gotta do and leave me alone. When I lived my life after Viet Nam, I would still be me, including my conscience.

I saw two guys with needles in their arms a couple of days after I sat on those sandbags smoking what turned out to be my last joint in Viet Nam. Seeing those assholes shooting up heroin scared the crap out of me. What were they doing? Apparently, drugs could be had fairly easily. Once or twice a week, someone would be quickly medevaced out to the hospital ship because of an overdose. I decided that pot was good and I actually enjoyed it, but I couldn't tolerate the fact that it could become a necessary crutch to get through the ordeal. After all, I made it through eleven months or so of missions to hell; I could certainly survive this pit of misfits disguised as Marines. And I must say that the marijuana highs weren't always an exhilarating or euphoric trip along ecstasy lane. Quite often I would end up with a downer. It was the trip along the long road to depression, anger, self-pity and even remorse. I remembered my discussion with the first sergeant and I remembered my father's and uncle's advice and thought of their sacrifice living through World War II. At the end of the day, they could look forward to a sane return home.

I cabbaged on to a smoking pipe of quite some grandeur. It was used by one of the potheads and left behind. It was on the sandbags outside the hooch or barracks. It was a beautiful briar pipe with the bowl carved in the shape of an old sailor's head. I kept it for a couple of days and since no one inquired about its disappearance, I gave it a good cleaning and elbow grease polish. I sent home for pipe cleaners and a couple of packages of pipe tobacco.

Thinking back on it now, I can only wonder what my mom and dad thought about their son being able to take up smoking a pipe in Viet Nam. But, nonetheless, I received my requested material along with three cans of my favorite boned chicken. Since I made no request for a specific tobacco, my dad sent two pouches of Granger. That was perfect. My Uncle Ed and Gramp smoked that old brand. I became a pipe smoker. Along with that came all the ribbing, jokes and laughing over the Recon dude with the pipe. He must think he's MacArthur or Einstein. Maybe he should get some cigars and pretend he's Churchill. They even wanted to borrow it to smoke "something decent" in it. My answer was emphatic, "Keep the fuck away from my pipe." I rather enjoyed it and I was pleased with myself for my continued separation from the pot haze.

I got into a rather pleasant habit by stumbling across a pretty good bunch of guys. My daily routine was working at the Comm. shack unpacking new PRC-25 radios and getting them ready for use. We also cleaned up and tested used equipment. Some of the radios were so shot, we scrapped them after stripping usable parts and logging in the serial numbers on an inventory sheet.

In the evening, eight or ten guys fired up a couple of radios. They knew which frequencies to tune into for stateside music. It was great. Somehow, they got patched into a radio station in Hawaii and others with high-range broadband capability. Another radio was used as a talk radio. Guys from other units would tune in to shoot the bull. It was fun to find someone from Connecticut or western Massachusetts to talk about home for a bit. We all took turns.

We'd all wander off from time to time to get a couple of beers from the club, go back to the Comm. shack and listen to real music. Most of the songs and groups I hadn't heard of but it was nice. My dad had sent me a package of Granger, a thin tin of Prince Albert, and a package of Carter Hall pipe tobacco. With them was a plastic bag. He suggested mixing them together in the bag. He said the mixture was pretty good and hoped the plastic bag would keep the tobacco from drying out. It was good and I enjoyed the smoke thoroughly. Some of the guys admitted that the pipe tobacco smelled good and some said their fathers smoked a pipe and it reminded them of home.

Even the nights were hot so the take-out beer didn't stay cold long. The radio stations talked about war protesters and all about demonstrations on college campuses. We didn't know much about it so all of that stuff was unclear to us. We listened with intent though when they talked about Nixon bringing home troops from Viet Nam. We wondered if it could really be true. We began to get our hopes up but told each other we shouldn't count on it. My time in country at that time was nearly twelve months. It was hard to believe I had been in Viet Nam a whole year. The Marines were the only service to require a 13-month "tour of duty" as it was called. All other branches of service were twelve months. My short-timer's calendar was really shaping up. I was starting to color in the little boxes on the upper thighs of my pin-up girl.

Guys were sending home souvenirs scrounged from grunt units they ran into. The grunts were infantry units that were typically battalion size. There was a lot of turnover. Guys were rotating out to go home or were killed or wounded. Replacements were getting hard to come by. As a result, they were pretty short-handed. They traded AK-47s which were Russian-made rifles used by NVA. The AK-47 was very similar to our M-16 rifles we used. And there were pistols, knives, personal belongings the grunts took off bodies.

Whatever souvenirs not sent home by the infantry guys were traded to the knuckleheads in the rear units like my Headquarters Battalion. The usual barter was pot, drugs and the good old U.S. dollar. It was free trade in a war zone like every other war, I suppose. Oddly enough, in Recon, all personal stuff we stripped off was turned in. Any guns, grenades and ammo on the bodies we stripped was just flung away, never to be found. We just couldn't take that stuff with us. Some of the knives or something special may have been kept but I was too naïve to think of that.

I didn't want any reminders of something I took off a person I killed, even if it was the so-called enemy. The hate for the enemy was drilled into us. Hate was also repeated a million times in our boot camp chant of "Kill VC, Kill VC" as we thrust the bayonet attached to our rifle into a straw replica over and over until it became a reality. The illusion was formed and our training was complete, except for one thing. In Nam, we killed to stay alive. It was the him or me mentality. No, there were no spoils of war for me. It was bad enough that we left bodies unclaimed and loosely covered in debris. There would be no souvenirs for me except for the sharp reminders in the middle of the night.

Our daily routine began to shape up as we prepared to close up shop. After cleaning and oiling radios and parts, they were packed away in crates. Next was the crane chopper that came for my two TSC-15 vans. At about that time, the official word was finally filtered down to our level. Gunny Bark held a formation one morning and went through his spiel about us. He reminded us we were not fit for his Marine Corps. We were sloppy misfits who looked like a ragtag bunch of bums. We couldn't stand straight and we didn't shine our boots. Our working utility uniform was not clean and ironed. Ironed? I wonder where he thought we'd get an iron.

It was 100 degrees every day. My shirt was an olive drab tee-shirt. Where would I pin my rank insignia? Eventually he ran out of insults and disgustedly announced the real purpose of the big early morning formation. We were being recalled, as he put it, from the Republic of South Viet Nam.

He talked like he was making a speech to the U.N. He couldn't just spit it out. He had to muster up the eloquence he pretended to have. One would think that President Nixon had personally called the gunny to relieve him of duty. Gunny Bark rambled on about how we had fulfilled our mission in northern I-Corps in Quang Tri province and were being reassigned to the Second Marine Division at Camp Lejeune in North Carolina. Stateside. We were already pretty sure that North Carolina was stateside but we listened on and on about how we would have to shape up or find ourselves in the brig.

Our departure would be piecemeal. We would not all be leaving together. I was assigned a date some two weeks in advance and was assigned to a sergeant and a dozen or so other guys to leave with a small caravan of radios and other Comm. equipment to Da Nang, where the ship *U.S.S. Iwo Jima* would transport us to California, where we would then be deployed to Camp Pendleton to blah-blah-blah. He just never needed to take a breath.

I felt lighthearted. I was actually going home for a twenty-day leave. I was alive and there was an excellent chance I would leave this place alive. It was a downer to have to go home on a ship. Most guys were sent home by air. It would take longer but I would get there. That was the important thing.

CHAPTER 23

Our nightly radio chatter on the net was nearing an end. We were burning through lots of batteries and since everything was getting packed away, our discussions on who was going home when and who to look up and keep track of and all the other promises that would be unfulfilled was quickly coming to an end.

On our last night of listening to music, radio talk and drinking beer, we had an unpleasant confrontation with the gunny. We were all around the two radios. One played stateside music relayed in from a broadcast in Da Nang. The other radio was our chatter box as we took turns transmitting and receiving talk with fellow Marines in nearby units from the states where we lived. It was fun to compare notes about where we each hung out or went to school or whatever. We were strangers one and all, yet having something in common at home lifted our spirits and was fun.

As usual, there were generally two to three guys smoking pot. I had just re-lit my pipe and popped open a beer that was lukewarm when out of nowhere a jeep came blasting up to us. We were hanging out in and around the Comm. shack. The jeep had its lights out and in a cloud of dust skidded to a stop right next to us. It scared the bejesus out of all of us.

The gunny jumped out of the driver's seat and ran right up to us. He was hollering and screaming in our faces.

"I've got you sons of bitches now. You pot-smoking bastards are busted. One last party, huh? Well, I got ya, every one of you. You potheads are a disgrace and I busted ya, every one of you. You're all going on report."

There was a sergeant in the passenger seat who slowly got out and just stood at the front of the jeep. He rested one foot behind him and stood with his arms crossed. He looked embarrassed. It was clearly the gunny's show. He was there just as a witness and probably to protect the gunny.

Gunny Bark started to bark louder, "So what do you have here, huh? Speak up, soon to be Private," he yelled in the face of one of the guys smoking pot.

"I can smell it, don't deny it. What's this, huh? Looky here what I've got."

He jammed his fingers into the shirt pocket of a pot smoker and pulled out the cellophane pack of joints.

"Aha, you like this stuff, do you? Well, it's mine now and you're on report. How about you, tough guy?" he spat out as he reached into another man's shirt pocket. He pulled out a small pipe used to pack pot in to smoke. "Nice little pipe. Just what I need. It's mine now. How 'bout that, tough guy?"

I could tell that the tough guy was about ready to take out the gunny. He looked pissed but never said a word. The sergeant in front of the jeep looked nervous. The gunny was on the verge of being snuffed out and the sergeant would have had to step in to try to save the old fool.

I had set my beer on the table behind the radio. I could just reach that far. We weren't allowed beer outside the club and I didn't want any trouble just a day or maybe two before I left. It was just then that the little barker walked right up to me and half-asked, half-remarked, "Is that beer yours?" He pointed to the beer behind the radio. "I saw the beer in your hand."

"Not me, Gunny," I lied. "It's just a beer someone must have brought from the club," I offered.

"You lying piece of shit," he spat out. "You Recon fucks are all the same. What's this you got here, Recon?"

Without warning he jerked the pipe out of my hand. I should have tossed the pipe behind me but I didn't think of it. I was doing nothing wrong. Well, I did have a beer, but a firing squad wasn't needed for that.

"So, Recon likes the pot, huh? Well, well. Who would think you're a pothead too?"

I tried to interject that it was just tobacco, not pot, but there was no reasoning with him. He was on a roll and having the time of his life. He was in charge and relished in his glory.

"Nice pipe, Recon. It will go nicely in my collection. What do you think of that? Like your pot now, do ya? You're going on report. All of you. I know who you all are. It will go in your file. There will be no end of tour award for all of you. You got that, you pot-loving misfits?"

With that and with my beautiful pipe in his right hand, he marched back to his jeep. With the sergeant sheepishly sliding into the passenger seat, the gunny roared the engine and with wheels spinning and dirt flying, he gunned the jeep into a semi-circle and sped off into the night. The air was filled with dust and dirt.

We all looked at each other in disbelief. What just happened? We didn't say a word. It was just incomprehensible that he would do that. At that moment, I thought that Gunny Bark was deranged. He wasn't

Gunny Bark anymore. Whatever his name was, from then on we only referred to him in the most profane way we could. He was called many vile names. My anger was intense.

As it turned out, I was whisked away the next afternoon in a caravan. That prick gunny never did have a chance to put anything in my file. My file was in a box on one of the trucks on its way to Da Nang. I would miss that pipe. My dad would have liked it too.

On the ride to Da Nang, it seemed safer than my journey to Quang Tri a year earlier. In the last year much had been done to improve the road and root out the VC who were lying in wait for an opportunity to strike. On my trip north to Quang Tri, the relentless rain poured on me. On my trip south, the sun scorched me and burned my brown skin. The breeze from the truck's movement felt good even though it was a hot furnace breeze.

I didn't even have a rifle. My trusty weapon had been turned in when I left Headquarters. I handed it to the Armorer at the supply shack. It was hard to let go. I had taken it apart, piece by piece, many times to clean it and oil each part with meticulous care. I slid many a magazine into the receiver. I've pulled the trigger many times to kill someone. It's had blood spilled on it, helicopter rides, and been carried up hills and mountains. It's been through firefights and rested by my cot for nearly a year. My rifle was always at my side like a favorite dog. I wondered where it went and who its next owner was. I hoped it would not lie in the mud next to a dead Marine.

The staging area in Da Nang was like a tent city. We arrived long after dark. There was no chow nor friendly faces to greet us. We were lost in a sea of confusion. We all knew to head for the guy who held the most paperwork, the one who yelled the loudest. I handed the big dude my orders. He ripped off the top sheet and told me to report to tent D-3. It was a big Red Cross tent. There were no bunks or blankets or moms to tuck us in. I found a spot nearest the opening and plunked down my seabag. It became my pillow. The ground was my bed.

The whole next day was a whirlwind of standing around, first in groups and then in better-defined groups. Magically, a slew of green U.S. Army buses appeared all in a neat line. It was a short ride to the docks.

We got on a Helicopter Ship (LPH-2). It was the *Iwo Jima*. The whole top deck was taken up by helicopters fastened down. There was a monstrous cargo bay below the deck with a large outside elevator to move the choppers around.

Naturally, I had never seen such a large ship, never mind been on one. My group was led two decks below for our sleeping quarters. Tiny bunks in a tiny room next to a tiny head (bathroom) was our digs. Our seabags were stowed away somewhere unknown to me. I sure hoped we wouldn't have to spend much time below in that place.

We took note of where we were and went back topside. When we came aboard, we missed it but later noticed boxes and boxes of soft-covered books. Some were used and most had the front cover torn off. Not only that, but there were boxes of cribbage boards and playing cards. All of the cribbage boards had defects but that was okay, I loved to play the game. Most guys didn't take a board, just the cards. That cribbage board was to stay with me for my lifetime. I still have it and have played hundreds of games. I taught many guys on the ship how to play and won a little money, too.

The captain was on the loudspeaker most of the afternoon, telling us Marines that we were guests aboard and how we would be made as comfortable as possible and to follow protocol and ship's rules. He told us repeatedly that we had a very limited supply of fresh water. Please take a ship shower, which was get wet, turn off the water and soap up, turn the water back on to quickly rinse off and get out. No one listened to that rule. We all hadn't taken a shower in real fresh water in so long we had forgotten what it was like. The food was plentiful, hot and tasted good. They ran out of ice cream on day three. The captain pleaded with us several times per day to please take ship showers. We were quickly running low on fresh water.

Marines were everywhere. There were even cots set up in the hanger deck. There was a good movie shown every night in the hanger deck. We just sat on the deck. It was great. It took very little time for our welcome to run out. Some of the guys got into fights with some of the Navy men. I felt bad for them. The Marines called them swabby boys and gave them a hard time. The sailors all had jobs to do and we were constantly in their way. We were using up their water, eating all the chow and creating havoc everywhere. Every day there was a detail of sailors assigned to railing duty. They had chains about two feet long and they wound them around the railing twice. They pulled back and forth to chafe the loose paint off the railing. Next was a work party to paint the railings. There was scraping and painting everywhere. Painting was a constant job aboard ship. I talked with the guys a lot as they were working. They asked about Viet Nam and what it was like. They were all service men just like us Marines, trying to do their job. The problems were always the Marines with a swagger and attitude that caused trouble.

My favorite pastime during the day was riding the waves. There was a group of us that hung out topside and went to the side rail. We had a tight grip on the rail. As the ship rode up a monster wave, the water seemed eye level and just below the deck. When the trough between the waves was there, it seemed like it was ten floors below us and we were atop a tall building looking down. We did that for hours. We'd play cribbage sitting on the deck in between our amusement at the rail. Another favorite pastime for me was reading. With the sunshine and sea breeze, I found a quiet corner somewhere to read a book. I was safe and alive. I also spent hours just looking out at nothing and thinking about home. There was no mail, of course. So, news to or from home was not possible.

I thought a lot about what to tell my family about what I did in Nam. I decided that I would make stuff up, boring stuff, so they would be interested. There was just too much I didn't want to talk about. They wouldn't understand anyway, so why bother. My dad might, but unless he was to pry, I'd keep it to myself. I knew he wouldn't pry too much.

Quite a few guys stayed below deck and were constantly sick. Some guys were topside, barfing over the rail. To me, the rhythmic sway and to and fro was pleasing and rather gentle. The heads were a mess. There were clogged toilets and drains with vomit on the deck mixed in with slime water and excrement. The poor sailors had to clean up one mess after another. Oh, how those guys hated the Marines. They were counting the days to get rid of us.

We detoured to Okinawa for water and resupply. The captain was hoarse from his hourly pleas for cooperation. Our officers were also trying to keep us busy and out of trouble. We had mandatory formations two to three times a day for calisthenics, drills and lectures. I was only a lance corporal so about everyone was my boss.

My favorite things seemed to involve me being alone, whether in my thoughts or reading. Being alone on the ship took creativity. After evening chow one day, I made a rather pleasant discovery. I took a tour to the boat's stern. I went all the way back to the fantail. Since we were on an easterly heading, I had a view of a spectacular sunset at sea. I was alone and it was almost quiet. Sitting on the warm deck, I was protected by the steel wall at my back. I could feel the power of the large engines as they groaned about their job. The vibrations from their immense power could be felt gently through the steel deck and through me. The propeller noise mingled with the engine's muffled drone. It could all lull one to sleep and it even did that a time or two. It was a perfect place to smoke a cigarette and read another Zane Grey or some mystery novel I traded for. The sunsets were never to be forgotten. The horizon seemed endless and the red, yellow and orange blaze blended into a sight to behold. Just as the galaxy of stars in Viet Nam, the spectacle of the sunset was testimony to God's presence.

How could such magnificent beauty be comingled with death and misery? It was a great deal to ponder. There would be no answer. It was above me, too vast for this human's knowledge. Yet I wondered where I could possibly fit in anywhere once I got home. I would have about eighteen months left of Marine Corps life, all of it probably at Camp Lejeune.

Maybe a career was in the cards. I quickly put away such thoughts on the future. I was likely not a good fit anywhere. What could I possibly do in life that could have any meaning at all, I thought. All thoughts about the future were pushed away. I hated those thoughts. I thought, and was even convinced, that I would never be in a normal life again.

Alone on that ship with too much time to think was probably not good. There was too much to try to sort out and too soon. I guess, like so many of us young guys, we saw and did so much, so fast, that it would take years to redefine normal. I would later learn that thousands of us soldiers of war would survive the battles and firefights only to have a mind that went haywire. So many went home only to be an empty shell, devoid of feelings and emotional stability. In a sense, they went to Viet Nam and never came back, almost as destructive as the 58,000 whose names are etched in black marble.

CHAPTER 24

It was obvious the ship was making circles in the vast ocean. The captain finally made an announcement about why we were delayed. Apparently, there was no berth for us at the docks and we would be delayed another six days. This business of ship travel was for the birds. It took us a total of twenty-two days to get to California from Da Nang.

A storm was intensifying. So was my toothache. My jaw was swollen and throbbing. No one was allowed topside nor was anyone anxious to be there. The ship heaved and swayed. Our berthing area and head smelled of vomit. I staggered my way through the narrow maze of passageways in search of sick bay. I stood in the long shifting line of Marines who were in search of something, anything to soothe their angry stomachs, sick from the rolling ship. I, on the other hand, suffered from an ailment whose relief would be more complicated. The ship's dentist sat me in his chair while he gripped the arm of the overhead light. He probed and jabbed for a solution, but alas, in vain.

"Lance Corporal, when I uncork that filling, I will have to remove decay and treat for an abcess. Obviously, I cannot do that in this storm. Take one of these pills every four hours and return here when things calm down."

"Yes, sir," I dutifully replied. Great. Happy pills for a day or two. Maybe the storm would end quickly.

It did not. My mouth was swollen and very painful. At the very first sign of a gentle sea, I found my way to the sick bay line. I believed the Marines had truly worn out their welcome aboard the *Iwo Jima*. The swabbies had had enough. Their patience was worn thin and I couldn't blame them. We didn't want to be there either. No one was happy.

I settled in the drillmeister's chair so grumpy-pants could re-evaluate the task at hand. Novacaine was used I guess, but when he pierced my gum to relieve pressure, the pus squirted out like shit from a goose. It gave me some relief but Doc's demeanor didn't lighten. He grumbled on about all my cavities and how proper brushing would have prevented all my problems. I hadn't had dental care in a year and I forgot to pack a toothbrush on all those missions. No gold star that day, for sure. I squirmed around in his chair for a good long while, enduring the drilling, probing and manipulation of my mouth. My pain seemed to be his pleasure, but after what seemed like many hours, he grumbled to a stop.

"This temporary filling will last a while, but not long. See a dentist when you get to wherever you're going. That's the best I can do under these conditions. Take these pills every four hours as needed for the swelling and pain. Don't come back for more."

"Yes, sir. Thank you, sir," I managed to say. I didn't recognize my own voice. My tongue and mouth and brain went in all different directions. Good grief.

I climbed up to my rack and fell asleep. I opted for soup and milk only for chow that day. Two of the guys saw me take a pill and asked if I wanted to sell any. Sure, why not?

"I'll give you fifty cents apiece, all ya got," was the offer. I counted out eighteen pills and folded them in a napkin. He handed me nine

U.S. dollar bills and just like that, I conducted my first and only drug transaction. I became a drug dealer on my way home from Nam. I had five more pills left over from my first visit to see Dr. Grump. I used them all.

Land ahoy! There was land ahead and the looming Bay Bridge. California! We got closer and closer and more excited and maybe even a little nervous. All our officers pretended they knew what to do but they seemed pretty confused. We were told to get in Company formations and then to line up here and there. Seabags were hoisted up from the hold, so we got in formation again to listen for our names. Then I got my worldly possessions which were all crammed into my familiar heavy olive drab canvas bag with a long strap and a clip at the top. That bag seemed to weigh 150 pounds and went everywhere we went just as our rifles did in Viet Nam. Next, we got in a single line that started at where the gang plank would be laid out and snaked around the decks and into the hangar deck. I wasn't at the very beginning of the line but pretty close. There were only about fifty guys ahead of me.

We were moving slowly at that point and could actually see people on the dock, lots of people. There was one open berth, which was ours. What a crowd there was. Imagine, all those people showed up at the Naval Shipyard to welcome us home. We could see that many of them had signs, too. We couldn't make out what they said but some of the guys thought maybe their families were there for a surprise welcome home. It seemed odd though because we were told to stay in line and there would be buses lining up to transport us to Camp Pendleton to get our orders for a duty station. We all knew we had twenty days leave coming to us first. We could see the buses next. It was exciting. The large ship crept around ever so slowly towards the dock. We were anxious to get the show moving. As we swung around to glide in to a stop, we could hear the crowd and began to see the writing on the signs. I was lucky enough to be at the right place to be a part of all the hoopla. Actually, the ship was secured rather quickly for all they had to do.

It was at that point that all of us returning warriors from the land of Nam began to see firsthand what the joyous celebration was all about. As we focused in on the signs being pumped up and down and sideways, and the screams became clearer, we realized it was no joyous reunion or welcome home at all. The handwritten signs with blood red paint drops on them were all so mean. Why? What the hell was happening?

The signs were hideous. Some signs said, "Baby Killers," "Murderers," "Go back, we don't want you," "War Mongers," "Rapists." There were others as well. The screams mingled together but reflected the sentiment of the signs. "We hate you," "Kill yourself." The screaming went on. Aboard ship, we slowly walked forward in a line, jointly shocked, dismayed and hurt. So, that was our welcome home.

As we began to disembark, the barrage of missiles began. They were hurling tomatoes, apples and oranges at us. Some guys got splattered by the tomatoes as they tore apart on the bulkhead next to us. I felt a hard thud on my right side and an orange rolled to the deck. I bent down and picked it up. As the barrage continued and the screams of hate intensified, I looked at the orange in my hand. It was a beautiful large orange. I hadn't seen an orange or a tomato or an apple in over a year. They were flung at us, not to give us a treat, but with the intention to hurt and humiliate us.

Most of the screaming mob were about my age. I held onto the orange and struggled ahead under the weight of my seabag. I looked straight ahead and tried to ignore their rants. Welcome home, Marines! We stuck together, as always. We filled up the buses and pulled away, one by one until the caravan passed through the front gate and on our way to that normal life that would be ahead in a far-away dream.

CHAPTER 25

No one said much on the bus. There wasn't backlash or laughter. There was no swearing and there could be no understanding. We were pretty much silent as we stared out the bus windows into the nothingness of being home. I ate the orange that was thrown at me. It was good. Third Recon had left Quang Tri to go to Okinawa but somewhere in the jungle of Nam, there were Marines in a desperate firefight with the North Vietnamese Army. Tonight, those Marines would long for the glorious day when they could once again step foot on the land of the USA, back to a normal life. Good luck with that, man.

We stood in more lines at Camp Pendleton. It was paperwork, digging out dress green uniforms from the seabag, sewing on chevrons with our new rank. I was a lance corporal. We pinned these small metal tags on the shirt, trousers and blouse (jacket). That identifying number was to keep everything straight when the whole bunch came back from the base cleaners.

Our two days were filled with spit-shining our shoes, haircuts, paymaster, and comparing our new duty stations. I would report to Camp Lejeune, Second Marine Division, Ontos Battalion. I knew that an Ontos was an obsolete small tank that had six gun barrels. I supposed that it was a kick-ass machine in its day, but modern warfare rendered it too bulky and ineffective in most terrain.

Late on the first day, I called home. My mom was emotional after I assured her that I really was in the United States and safe in California.

I told her I would be released to go on twenty days leave in three or four days. I didn't tell her that I would be free to go in a day or two and that I would be going to San Diego. I promised my team leader, John, that I would visit him and his family when I returned from Nam. John was a civilian again and looking forward to my visit.

One of our pastimes in Quang Tri base camp was to talk about our families and home. We bragged about everything. Of course, we all had the best mom who was the best cook. "I want a big turkey dinner with a tall glass of milk when I get home." "Not me," someone would say, "I can't wait for my mom's meatloaf and mashed potatoes, red potatoes." One day John piped in, "No one can make pancakes from scratch like my mom." He was always talking about his mom's pancakes.

The next day, a taxi took me to the Greyhound bus terminal and I sat alone in my seat once again staring out of a window. It was a long ride to San Diego. I felt guilty not going home right away. I wanted to see John again, but I wasn't really looking forward to seeing him as a civilian. Our bond was of Marine war buddies. We were Recon. I just couldn't picture him as a civilian.

My instincts were right. When he picked me up at the bus terminal, I almost didn't recognize him. His hair was down over his ears and neck in a scraggly mess. He wore dirty jeans and sandals. His shirt was gaudy and misshapen. But I couldn't mistake that big ol' ear to ear grin of his.

Our greeting was warm. We both talked at the same time, not knowing what the other was saying. I wanted to get the first jabs in. He was a squared-away team leader, kick-ass Recon machine turned into a grubby run-of-the-mill hippie in no time. I razzed him to a fair-thee-well. He assured me he would fit in at the party he had planned for that night better than I would. That, too, was debated.

John's mom and dad were very nice and respectful. Me, not so much. I told them that they should thank me for keeping their sorry-ass son alive. His mom looked at me like she was informed that it was quite the other way around. I dialed it down a turn or two and all went well from there. When his mom asked about breakfast the next morning, I quickly answered pancakes. I told her of the many stories and their son's braggart behavior, respectfully, of course.

John's driving was reckless, risky and riled my stomach. He had a pattern of weaving and speed. The city streets seemed to challenge his intellect. Our slow, well-thought-out steps in the jungle was a thing of the past, I supposed. We went to some night club downtown and met some of his friends. The music was loud and clouds of smoke prevented much breathing. He did all the introductions and I met his girl. I wondered where he had found her. She laughed at everything and giggled as we did in third grade when Mrs. Metcalf's slip was showing. John seemed to like it and they danced to weird music that was much too loud. We couldn't even talk. I found a stool at the bar and lit an unfiltered Camel to add to the pollution. My glass of scotch was cold and I marveled at the wonderful invention of the ice cube. Never again would I take ice for granted. I took my scotch on the rocks in long sips and dragged deeply on the cigarette. Looking around at the dancing and laughter, I wondered if I would have to live like this, too. I hoped not.

"Come on, buddy," John coaxed, "Loosen up, relax, have some fun."

"I am, this is great," I lied. "You've got it made with all the chicks and the good life." I heaped on the crap, hoping he would believe me and leave me be.

I danced with some chick with long beads and short, bleached hair. She stared at me with serious eyes. I think she wanted me to mount her right then and there. She raised her arm, took a drag from a joint and passed it to me. I took a hit and gave it right back. I didn't want to go where she was quickly headed. I did want another scotch, though. Cutty Sark was my friend.

I made it through the ordeal. John and I had a pretty quiet ride to his home. I made up my mind that I would leave for home the next day. He understood my desire to go home.

His mom's pancakes were good but I missed real syrup. Log Cabin syrup? Really? Undercooked bacon and instant coffee completed the meal. Even undercooked, it was the first bacon I'd had in over a year and tasted good.

John took me to the airport and we made our promises to keep in touch. Actually, we did keep in touch. For many, many years John called me every Christmas Eve. And then John called one day to announce he was coming to the East Coast with friends and he'd like to stop by. So, 42 years after our time together in Viet Nam, we crossed paths again.

I was shocked to see my old Recon buddy at the door. I guess I expected him to look like he did in 1968. Boy was I wrong. He turned into a blimp-sized, rotund giant. His face was mottled with dark red blotches and he wore a black sea captain's hat that he probably won at the circus midway. He even sounded different, gravelly and short of breath. But that smile, that give-away broad smile shone through. We gave each other a big bear hug. Luckily, he didn't break any of my ribs. He then thrust a bottle wrapped in an old paper bag at me and hinted that we should have a toast. There was no need for a corkscrew. The screw cap of the cheapest bottle of what the label said was wine opened easily.

We sat up half the night. That poor guy had been practically homeless for years. He got by, shifting from friend to friend for a place to live. He scared me by suggesting he was thinking about living out our way for a few months. I stammered out some reasons why he wouldn't like it. His health was poor. He had had heart attacks and lung problems. I felt so badly for him. He had been married once for a short while. I knew we were at the pinnacle of health and strength in Nam but I thought it was extraordinary that his life would turn out so badly. When John left, we took pictures, hugged and made new promises. That was 18 years ago and I haven't heard from him since we waved when he drove away. I fear the worst and miss my old friend.

The airport was busy but I was able to get tickets. Of course, I was military stand-by and would be allowed on the plane only if there was an empty seat. I missed two flights and on the third I think the agent felt sorry for me so she assured me I would have a seat on the next plane to Chicago and from there to Bradley Field. I found a phone booth and called home collect to tell them I would be at Bradley at 4:00 pm. My mom assured me they would be there to meet me.

I was nervous. It wasn't the queasy feeling like when the chopper is heading into an LZ to drop us off, it was more like the proverbial butterflies in the stomach. I knew they wanted me home. I knew they loved me and missed me and worried about me in my absence. I wondered how my brother and sister had changed. I hoped they wouldn't mention Viet Nam. I wondered if they would think I've changed. I lost weight, that's for sure.

The plane ride was long and boring. I bought a magazine to read. I, in my uniform, didn't attract any attention, good or bad. No one spat at me nor did anyone offer a handshake or thanks for your service. I was as invisible as a homeless vet on a busy city street corner.

As we approached Connecticut and Bradley Field, I got butterflies in my throat. I pretended to read, but my mind was back in Nam. I rushed from the landing in Da Nang in the pelting rain to my first firefight to leaping into a chopper taking relentless enemy fire. Everything blended together and merged into a heart-pounding moment of self-induced fear. I think I was afraid to go home. I was afraid it would be different and afraid it would be the same.

The lumbering approach to the airport over the treetops was clumsy. The wings rocked up and down in adjustments to the wind. I longed for the chopper. It would have been a straight shot in, fast and sure. The touchdown and bounces again reminded me of Da Nang. It seemed like a long time ago, even a lifetime. Yes, it really was a lifetime. My mind was cluttered and inconsistent. I couldn't sort out reality. I was home again, for sure. All would be well, I repeated over and over again.

Military stand-by means you get that last seat in the most undesired location. I would be the last to exit the plane. Slowly walking down the aisle, passing seat after empty seat, my mind raced. I remember being so nervous I ducked my head slightly crossing through the doorway and stepped onto the top platform of the stairs. The sun shone in a late afternoon warmth. The air was crisp and clear and filled with the sweet smell of Connecticut air. I paused to look around.

On the corner of the tarmac near the terminal door stood my family. All were staring at the last man to disembark the plane. I raised my arm in a faint wave in recognition of their presence. Their Marine was home.

EPILOGUE

Hugs and kisses were had by all. Mom was a little weepy but Dad, brother, sister and girlfriend were not.

I got all the usual questions about the previous year. I evaded most of them quite well. Dad was, for the most part, pretty quiet. Brother and sister were the most inquisitive and were easy to dodge. Girlfriend may have felt uncomfortable and like her presence was expected. Mom took it all in, looking for signs of change and asking motherly questions. It was all so foolish, I thought. We were talking about things like I had been away at college and was home for Christmas break. The best news I got was that Mom was making a full turkey dinner the next day. The worst news was that my girlfriend's Gram had a bad stroke and was doing poorly. Dad wasn't paying attention and went north instead of south on the Interstate. But we made it home eventually.

Home. It was that little space in the vast world I had longed for, dreamed about and missed so much in the past year. And there it was.

Once inside, everyone busied themselves with chores and Mom started to cook. My girlfriend went home. I lugged my seabag up the stairs, turned right and walked into my room. My old domain looked undisturbed. I wasn't happy, sad, relieved or emotional. I was a little numb and detached. There on the nightstand was my senior yearbook with my cap tassel. All the knick-knacks were lined up on the shelves. They all had some meaning and story at some point in another life. The drawers held my clothes, all neatly pressed and folded. They would all be way too big for me now. Mom picked up on that right away at the airport. "Didn't they feed you over there?" she wondered out loud.

I undressed and lay down on the bed. The bed was so soft and the two pillows seemed to be too much. I lay still and stretched out. I wondered what had happened to my Civil War cot with the blood stains where my shoulder rested. I reviewed the possibilities in my mind. In the background, I heard talking. The voices were all so familiar and comforting.

I fell asleep, safe in my own bed.

CAMP LEJEUNE

Camp Lejeune was as advertised. It was a very large, sprawling base for the Second Marine Division under the command of Major General Michael P. Ryan. I was assigned to the Second Anti-Tank Battalion. My Military Occupational Specialty (MOS) was 2531, Radio Operator. As such, I was under a master sergeant in the Comm. shack. We had all the various radios, antennas and specialty gear, both stationary and mobile, ready to go at a moment's notice anywhere in the world to be the Division Central Communications Command.

We had quite a few radio operator Marines straight out of Comm. school who needed a great deal of training on advanced radio technology, and training in all applications of use. I was an instructor. The Marine Corps was in the process of disbanding the Ontos and we were tearing out the Comm. units from the tanks for inventory, parts and deep six (trash).

One day a reporter with the *Camp Lejeune News* stopped by to ask the master sergeant permission to interview me. They did a big spread on me and my experience in Nam. The word was out. Up until then, no one knew anything about me, as it should have been. We were all Marines working together. I did not like being singled out. All the hoopla was part of the preparation for the huge celebration to take place. The Second Marine Division was about to celebrate its twenty-nine-year anniversary. Most of the 22,000 Marines on the base would take part in an awards ceremony in the gigantic field house. Generals, past and present, would all be there. Exhibits, field exercises, VIP tours, banquet and the Commanding General's Ball would take place on 5 February 1970.

I got word to report to the battalion sergeant major. Now what, I thought. Once again, I had truly forgotten about the Navy Cross thing. The sergeant major fell all over himself heaping praise on me and how fortunate they were to have a Marine like me and what an honor it will be for me to be awarded the Navy Cross at the ceremony in front of 22,000 Marines and half the generals and brass in the Northern Hemisphere.

"What are you talking about, sir?" I asked. I was puzzled about the whole thing. I figured that when I got to Camp Lejeune, the company Captain would pin on the medal at Monday morning formation and be done with it. What's all this?

The sergeant major went on to explain that the Commanding General of Camp Lejeune, Major General Michael P. Ryan was planning a big anniversary celebration and it would add to the whole celebration to award such a high decoration. The Commanding General of FMF (Fleet Marine Force) Atlantic, himself, would pin the medal on me. Sergeant major wanted the names and addresses of my family so General Ryan could invite them personally. All travel expenses would be paid and they would stay as long as they wanted in the VIP quarters of the base guest house. Military VIP had special officers' quarters to enjoy.

I explained that my family would be confused because I didn't mention the Navy Cross thing when I got home.

"You what?" boomed the sergeant major, in his big sergeant major voice, "You didn't 'MENTION' it?" he emphasized.

"No, sir," I replied. "I didn't want to get into the whole thing. And besides, it would have upset my mother for no real reason."

A thin smile of understanding briefly exposed his thoughts. But he reverted back to his stern appearance. He was short and thin but all muscle. His voice boomed and he puffed up and had a little bounce when he bellowed. It was all an act but it scared the bedazzle out of Marines who didn't know him. I could see through his act but treated him with the utmost respect that he well deserved. Already I liked him a lot.

He proceeded to admonish me in his practiced powerful voice, "VanCor," he said, "Do you really mean to tell me you've told no one about your heroism and the Navy Cross medal?"

"Yes, sir. I've told no one."

"Well, I'll be goddamned. I've never heard of such a thing. Well, if that were me, I'd be out there with a bullhorn. Well, I'll be damned. Wait till the general hears this. He won't believe it."

I didn't respond, but I gave him the information he asked for and started to leave.

"Oh, report to the Battalion quartermaster at 1500 hours. You'll be fitted for a set of dress blues. You've got to look presentable for that big old Navy Cross medal."

"Yes, sir," I replied in leaving. Oh boy, I would have some explaining to do now after my mom and dad read the invitation letter from the big man himself.

I was a little evasive to the inquiries but the family would come, along with my girlfriend, Cherie, for the ceremony. The days and weeks passed in preparation. All of Lejeune was abuzz. It broke up our routine work schedule and the boredom of little to do.

I was taking a lot of ribbing from the guys. The nearest big town to Lejeune was Jacksonville, NC. There was the annual push for fundraising for United Way. Camp Lejeune was a big sponsor of that and I was asked to be the representative for a radio commercial. After a few takes, the commercial to plug United Way was aired. It not only aired but was played what seemed like every fifteen minutes. All the guys were imitating me and could do the ad from memory. "Norm is going to be a big star." "Hell, he is now. All the brass loves him." "He'll be on Armed Forces radio soon." "Nah, he'll go straight to the movies. He'll be bangin' Jane Fonda and living in a mansion." And so it went on and on but all in good fun.

As the big day approached, I participated in a big rehearsal in the Field House. What a cavern. It was huge. There was a big stage set up with a set of stairs to climb. I learned where to go when the band started with the USMC hymn. I learned all the about faces and executions. Good grief. I was actually getting a little nervous. All the PR folks took the whole thing so seriously.

The evening before the big event, I drove down to the main gate to await the arrival of my family. They were expected and were on the list to pass through the gate and to the visitor's center. When they arrived, we all hugged. They were tired, as expected. I escorted them to the VIP quarters. I didn't know ahead of time, but a Captain met us there and was assigned to my family for the entire stay, to take them everywhere and accommodate all their needs.

When I arrived at the Field House and entered the next morning, 5 February 1970, my family was already seated and the Marines were still filing in. The place was packed. Imagine a whole division, 22,000 U.S. Marines, all seated, in that mammoth place. I waved to my family but was escorted to my seat next to the stage. I never saw so many stars in my life. I didn't know there were that many Marine Corps generals. Plus, some Army brass were there too. They all must have been old buddies with General Ryan. They all had gray hair and looked like they came out of the same mold. It was a sight to behold.

The band played, speeches were made and introductions were made. I almost fell off my chair when General Omar Bradley was introduced. Not only was the old boy there with his wife, but when he stood up and waved, he was seated in the front row right next to my mom and dad. The famous general from WWII who, with Patton and Eisenhower, won the war against Germany, was right there next to my family. One of the greatest generals in the history of warfare was with my parents! That really pumped me up.

The big FMF General Kahoona stepped to the microphone on the gigantic stage and commenced to read a long citation about me and the highlights of the firefight and me carrying out my wounded comrades. I hadn't heard of or seen the citation before. When he finished, the band started playing the Marine Corps hymn, which was my cue to climb the stairs and jigger myself here and there like I had been told. I did all that, snapped a sharp salute to General Kahoona and stood at attention front and center. He jabbered some about the exemplary example of Marine Corps honor and tradition and, with great pleasure and distinction, it was his privilege to award me the Navy Cross on behalf of the President of the United States, the Secretary of the Navy and the United States Marine Corps. As he finished his spiel, he pinned the heavy Navy Cross medal on my dress blues and we saluted. The entire Marine division and guests rose to their feet in a thunderous ovation. It was truly overwhelming.

As I marched down the stairs, I swear to God that my mind was in the middle of an ambush firefight in Viet Nam and carrying out two Marine Recons. I wished with every ounce of my heart that Second Lieutenant John Shinault and Lance Corporal Daniel Tirado could still be alive. There would be no medal, no hoopla. But it wasn't meant to be. The deed was done. They were dead, I lived and the two guys I carried out lived. Marines lived, they died and they took care of each other. That's just what they did.

The ceremony soon ended and the Marines began the orderly exit. The captain houseboy and a Navy League representative greeted me to escort me to my family. My father was beaming and Mom still had tears in her eyes. She wiped at tears while we hugged. She said she didn't know what to do when General Kahoona read the citation - cry or get sick. I think she did both. Brother and sister didn't say much but were probably proud of big brother. It would undoubtedly pass soon. My girlfriend thought the whole event was pretty cool.

It was then that General Ryan intervened and introduced me to General Omar Bradley. I was speechless and said "Sir" a lot. Captain houseboy and the Navy League guy were trying to steer us to an alcove where a photographer awaited the entourage for pictures.

As I walked across the floor with General Bradley, he said, "Young man, during my career I've been awarded five Navy Cross medals. All five of them together don't measure up to your one." Oh, how I wished I had known ahead of time that he would be there. Afterward I thought of so many things I could and should have said. I simply thanked him and said I didn't think what he said was true.

And then, something happened I shall always regret. As we were all posing for pictures, all of the big boys with stars on their shoulders filed out with General Bradley. General Ryan graciously stayed for a moment to pose with me. I have always regretted not asking General Bradley to stand with me and my father. What a wonderful picture and memory that would have been. No doubt, General Ryan had a very special luncheon for all the muckity-mucks, which was appropriate. As for us, we had a private luncheon served in the VIP quarters with the sergeant major and some of the lesser VIPs like the battalion commander and the Navy League folks. It was a very special affair followed by a guided tour in a fancy USMC car of some staged field exercises, up close inspection of weapons and vehicles and the TSC-15 van, which I explained.

The culmination of the day, following a lovely dinner, was an evening parade at the very large parade field. We had special seats in the grand review section but not with General Ryan and his group. That was fine and as it should have been. It was a tiring and long day.

The sergeant major gave me a special three-day pass so I could travel with my family to Washington, D.C. to take in all the sights we could. It was special for Mom and Dad because their honeymoon had been in Washington.

I was promoted to corporal and then sergeant, both meritoriously. The sergeant major and I became as close as could be expected, given the difference in rank. He had me in his office frequently and gave me many special assignments involving trust and the use of my secret clearance. I looked up to him.

It was he who encouraged me to go to Greece to participate in the NATO War Games. Being a sergeant, I led a team of specially trained Marines on the first assault wave, climbing down nets over the side of a ship and going ashore in the same landing crafts used in WWII. Going over the side of a battleship with a heavy pack and rifle was scary. No one fell. We set up crypto radio equipment so the commanders could converse without the mock enemy being able to understand the scrambled voice communication.

We had a blast in the Alexandropolis countryside, seeing 1,000-year-old olive trees. We spent time in Athens after the war games and then on to Naples, Italy and Barcelona, Spain, through the Strait of Gibraltar and back to Lejeune. It was a two-month adventure.

Upon my return, the sergeant major spoke with me often about re-enlistment. We had many discussions about a Marine Corps career. He made a lot of sense.

He also arranged a short meeting with us and General Ryan in the big boy's office suite. That was a real honor. General Ryan made a pitch that was hard to refuse. He offered many perks and gave me the long version of the argument to stay in. He ended by telling me that if there was anything he could ever do for me, just ask. I was very humbled by his sincere words.

I came very, very close to re-enlisting and there have been many times in my life that I've wondered what life would have been like for me in the Marine Corps. What I wouldn't have, though, is my two beautiful children, Christine and Kimberly. Their lives, with their two special men and grandchildren, make me realize that I've done well. I married that girlfriend to make it all happen.

So, on 15 January 1971, on a cold, snowy morning in a quiet office in Camp Lejeune, N.C., I signed my name and my life in the United States Marine Corps came to an end, just like that.

My days in the Marine Corps were over but my nights in Viet Nam were not. And then the nightmares began.

PHOTOGRAPHS

Advanced Infantry Training
I am on the left with Southington High School buddy, Jimmy Warnat.

Weekend respite from Radio School in San Diego.
Enjoyed the beach at La Jolla, south of San Diego.

Robert Jenkins at ammo dump. He was with team next to me (3-C-1).
Jenkins was killed on his next mission and posthumously awarded the Medal of Honor.

Lieutenant John Shinault. He was killed May 7, 1969.

Interior of gunship that accompanied all insertions and extractions from jungle LZ's.

Typical view of jungle terrain on our way to the insertion LZ.
Every single insertion comes with a sick feeling of anticipation.

Last minute preparations before choppers landed to take us for jungle insertion.

Recon Team at base camp with tiger that attacked them.

Tiger skin drying in the sun.

Me about five months of Recon in-country.

Two teams going out on missions that morning.
My team in rear—Juan, John (team leader), me, Nick. Bart was on R&R.
Fewer men, quieter movement.

Villager on the path from a Recon dump with food for the family,
walking through a cemetery.

Point man, Bart, on left.

I am in the foreground with Bart at top with team leader John to his left.
Just before dark. We were tired, hungry, thirsty and fearful of the jungle black nights.

Robert Jenkins and Danny Tirado, on right.
Danny was right behind me when he was killed May 7, 1969.

Heading to the "Rock Pile" - Sierra relay station. It was a mountaintop radio relay position we manned for about a week, over Christmas, 1968.

I built this little collapsible bunk at the "Rock Pile."
It had to be collapsed when a chopper came in with re-supplies.
I am opening a box from home – largest I ever received.

Sitting on the precarious perch of our latrine at the "Rock Pile."
Note the C-ration box and litter that fed the rats.

Guys waiting in line at the mess hall. Third from right is Danny Tirado.

John and me as chopper was landing.

Juan speaking with John just prior to insertion.

Heading in to India relay station, a remote mountaintop where we had a radio station to communicate between Headquarters and teams in the jungle.

Me with team in chopper going in, studying terrain from 500 feet.

Left to Right: John, me, Bart, Nick, and Ted with Juan and Gary in front

Twice during my Recon days, we got a pallet of warm beer (two cans each). This photo is right after a mission and shower of muddy river water. 3-C-2 with two friends.

Left to Right: John, Bart and Lieutenant Shinault

We were in razor sharp elephant grass. It was noisy and you couldn't see ahead of you. Very scary terrain. We avoided it whenever possible.

Some of the guys with the pilot and crew counting all the bullet holes and broken rotor after we almost crash-landed. We never made it to the tarmac.

*Ah, mission complete, extraction successful and on our way home
to base camp in Quang Tri. Me and Doc McKeon.*

Memorial Service for First Lieutenant John Shinault and Corporal Danny Tirado.

My new home at Headquarters Battalion
after I left Recon to operate the TSC-15 van radio.

Perspective photo of TSC-15 van.

Standing in doorway looking inside my TSC-15 van radio.
This is where I had my first marijuana.

*Rickety derelicts from history. This collection of generators powered
the TSC-15 van radio I used in Headquarters Battalion.*

What's left of a village cemetery. Note the scattered pieces of stone.
Most of the stone grave markers have been destroyed through the years.
This view is near the TSC-15 van radio in Headquarters Battalion.

First view of our homecoming "Welcome" from aboard the U.S.S. Iwo Jima.

Rather poor quality but it shows the enormity of the Field House.
Perspective of the stage and where my family was seated (left front).
General Bradley and his wife had not been introduced yet.

The generals with the most stars are on the stage. I am seated to the right of the stage. General Omar Bradley, his wife and my dad are shown seated on the far right. The men lined up are either facing a firing squad or about to receive decorations.

Left to Right:
General Omar Bradley, Mrs. Bradley, Lawrence VanCor, Merilda VanCor, Cheryl Kupa, and Marie VanCor. My brother Kenneth is just out of the picture to the right.

Left to Right:
Marie, Mom ("Tillie"), Kenneth, me (with my big ol' Navy Cross medal),
Dad ("Larry"), Cheryl ("Cherie")

CPSIA information can be obtained
at www.ICGtesting.com
Printed in the USA
BVHW092331181220
595982BV00012B/26/J

9 781628 062984